MW00648006

THE BOOKS OF
KAHLIL GIBRAN

"His power came from some great reservoir of spiritual life else it could not have been so universal and so potent, but the majesty and beauty of the language with which he clothed it were all his own."   CLAUDE BRAGDON

The Madman	1918
Twenty Drawings	1919
The Forerunner	1920
The Prophet	1923
Sand and Foam	1926
Jesus the Son of Man	1928
The Earth Gods	1931
The Wanderer	1932
The Garden of the Prophet	1933
Prose Poems	1934
Nymphs of the Valley	1948
Spirits Rebellious	1948
A Tear and a Smile	1950

∵

This Man from Lebanon: *A Study of Kahlil Gibran by Barbara Young*

PUBLISHED BY ALFRED A. KNOPF

THIS MAN
FROM LEBANON

Kahlil Gibran

THIS MAN
FROM LEBANON

A STUDY OF
KAHLIL GIBRAN

BY

BARBARA YOUNG

1971

NEW YORK : ALFRED·A·KNOPF

THIS IS A BORZOI BOOK
PUBLISHED BY ALFRED A. KNOPF, INC.

All rights reserved under International and Pan-American Copyright Conventions. Published in the United States by Alfred A. Knopf, Inc., New York, and in Canada by Random House of Canada Limited, Toronto. Manufactured in the United States of America and distributed by Random House, Inc., New York.

Copyright, 1945 by Barbara Young
Published January 15, 1945
Reprinted Fifteen Times
Seventeenth Printing, September 1971

TO

MARIANNA GIBRAN

There is a race of Strangers, of Wayfarers, that persists upon the Earth. They dwell with us awhile, calling us brothers, but we come to be aware that they are of an immortal stuff somewhat more deific than ourselves, and only insofar as we receive and comprehend their utterance, only insomuch as we join our wavering, uncertain voices with their voice, may we partake in brief and finite measure of their communion.

When we write of these, we would that we might dip our quill in light, not ink. We would wish to write of them with pure truth, not with platitude. Better still, we would wish to sit at the feet of remembrance, writing only when the marvel of their power and wisdom shall strike fire from the fagots of our silent heart, and when our writing shall be a flame upon the surrounding night.

B. Y.

FOREWORD

It is far from my desire to write anything so formidable as a biography of Kahlil Gibran.

I do wish to write as simply and directly as possible of the Gibran I knew, the man among his friends, in his studio at work with pencil or brush, the tireless one, the one who was ready sometimes with singing and laughter, always with quick understanding and instant recognition of good work from the pen of a fellow worker, and with the unerring finger to point out a failure to record "the inevitable word in the inevitable place."

To write revealingly of him is not a matter of rehearsing the events and circumstances of his life and its achievements or the order of these events. No facts, no assembly of facts, no recital of incidents and experiences can give any true conception of the reality of Gibran. He was one of the rare gestures of the Mighty Unnameable Power, and in his voice and his being were vested an authority not to be confounded with mere human excellence, for he was never wholly and entirely in this world.

The reasons and laws that govern ordinary men do not govern genius. Gibran's mother said of him in his youth, "My son is outside of psychology." Never was there a truer word. She knew in her blood and in her breath what brain would never have discovered. It was knowing, not knowledge.

Gibran would sometimes say, after long moments of preoccupation with some thought apparently far removed from the present time and place, "Forgive me. So much of the time I am not here." And one being with him for hours at a time, day after day, grew accustomed to this withdrawal, recognized and respected it.

To sit in his presence through this frequent silence which descended upon him was an exaltation of the spirit. The vibration of the room heightened perceptibly, and a sense of unearthly import lay upon the air. One held one's breath, fearful of breaking in upon his sanctuary. And the return to the present seemed always an effort of the will.

For seven years, and up to the very moment of his death, I had the joy and privilege of knowing Gibran as poet and painter, and as a close and beloved friend. Seven years of friendship and work; as he so generously said, we were "poets working together in Beauty's name."

Gibran held the firm belief that there is nothing small in this earthly life, nothing by chance. He called it the "continuity of life," and by this he meant this present, as well as all periods of existence that become the vessel for the human spirit both now and hereafter. It is all in the Pattern, all in the inevitable Design.

Therefore it was not by chance that when *The Prophet* was read for the first time in public, at St. Mark's In-the-Bouwerie in New York City on an autumn afternoon in 1923, I sat in the crowded church and listened to the reading by Butler Davenport, that distinguished gentleman of the theatre.

I did not know until long afterward that the author of that amazing book sat also in the church, listening to his words as they fell upon the hearts of hundreds of utterly silent people.

I knew only that I had heard startling and essential truth spoken with a power and a beauty that I had never heard or read anywhere up to that moment.

It was inevitable that I should have a copy of the book for my own, and that I should share it immediately with others, many others. Inevitable too, that I should write, after a time, to the poet to express, however inadequately, what depth and height and vastness his *Prophet* had added to my consciousness; and then his gracious invitation to come to his studio "to talk about poetry" and to see the pictures.

So I went to the old West Tenth Street building, climbed the four flights of stairs and found him there, smiling, welcoming me as though we were old friends, which we soon found that we were, very old friends indeed.

We hear often the assertion that any estimate of the spirit and substance of an artist's work is of value only insofar as it approaches the work from an impersonal point of view.

Repetition does not make truth. It would be impossible, certainly, for me to take an entirely impersonal view of Gibran's poetry and painting. I have found it possible, however, through the years to stand aside from the personal relationship, and to explore the fabric of this man's genius with an impartial regard, the more so, I sincerely believe, because of intimate knowledge of his working self gained at close hand.

It is a fact that I had become steeped in his work before I knew the man himself. I had come to him through his poetry, not to the poetry through him. My position had already been taken, and it has never changed.

His own attitude was of great assistance. He knew that it was my purpose to write of him. He knew that the writing must not be overinfluenced by the devotion of friendship. He knew also, the more from occasional differences of opinion when one or the other would say, "Over my dead body shall you publish that line," that my integrity as a writer would not permit any softness or sentiment to impair the estimate of his great work.

During his lifetime when I was about to depart upon some journey, to some distant city where I would read from the "black books" and speak of the author, he would say, "When you stand up before the people you are to forget that you are my friend." And it became increasingly possible, not to forget, but to put aside, the remembrance of that friendship, and to speak as impersonally as before our meeting. The power and authority of the utterances contained between the covers of the books overshadowed every other feeling for the time being, and this was well.

In 1931, a few months after Gibran had finished this span of life, I wrote a slender brochure about this man from Lebanon. It was in response to hundreds of inquiries: "Where can we read something about him?" There had been nothing written in English except the briefest of articles.

The brochure was written under stress during a period of deep personal sadness and exacting activity in the matter of caring for the precious effects left in the studio where Kahlil Gibran had lived for eighteen years. The many things that had been dear to his heart, and also dear to the hearts both of the multitude of his friends and of strangers who had visited him through the years and had become no longer strangers — all these were to be packed and sent, at his request, to his home town of Bsherri in Lebanon.

There were literally hundreds of drawings and paintings. Probably as many as half of them even I had never seen, and they were stored on an upper balcony, row upon row, in a sad condition of dust and neglect. But there were young and ready hands to come to the task: several faithful and devoted young Lebanese and Americans to whom the labour was at once a joy and a grief, but always a privilege, were constantly at my side until all was completed.

At that time I wrote: "We are still too near to Gibran in terms of time and space to set down the drama of his life upon the page. The Earth still looks for the magic of his presence when her door opens, and the sound of his voice still lingers in her ears."

Thirteen years have passed and I do not wish to change one of those words. I wish to emphasize that neither has the magic of his presence ever been withdrawn nor has the sound of his voice failed in the ears of the listeners.

From the four corners of the Earth the word still comes: "Gibran is more alive to us than ever." "During these ghastly days his words steady my heart when it falters with unbearable grief." "The Book lies beside me on my bed-table, and I never sleep without reading something to take with me into the darkness of the terrible night."

So, here is the book. Not a life of Gibran, not a chronological record. He said, "Telling you what I have done is not telling you what I am."

This book is not a rehearsal of genealogy, not a family tree. It is a simple story of the great man as I found him during the seven years that immediately preceded his death, the years when his gifts and his consciousness were at their height; the great man who was also simple in his tastes and desires as Earth is simple; who was at home in the above-world but never quite at home upon this planet, and who burned with the flame of a tireless passion of divine life that encompassed the fagots of his body and consumed him at last.

What he had to say, his contribution to the world of painting and literature, both Arabic and English, is immeasurable. Yet these contributions are not the summit of the mountain that Gibran scaled. His greatest and most enduring masterpiece was traced neither with pen on paper nor brush on canvas, but with his deathless spirit upon the spirit of the race.

His spoken words, the wisdom of his counsel, the contagion of his infinite faith in God, the Most High, God, the Father of all living, his boundless love and understanding and compassion for all men, sons of the Father — these have enriched countless multitudes of lives to their eternal treasure, and the lives of their children's children.

If he had never written a poem or painted a picture his signature upon the page of the eternal record would still be inerasable. The power of his individual consciousness has penetrated the consciousness of the age, and the indwelling of his spirit is timeless and deathless.

This is Gibran.

B. Y.

Sharon, Connecticut
April, 1944

CONTENTS

ILLUSTRATIONS

THIS MAN
FROM LEBANON

I

"I WAS A SMALL VOLCANO"

There is a great tempest raging in the sky, torrents
of rain are falling upon the Earth, the trees are beaten
about in a great wind, as I sit down to write these words
about Kahlil Gibran, this man from Lebanon. It is an
omen of good for the book. There was in this man from
early childhood a passion for storms. There was something in him, he said, that was released, unharnessed
and set gloriously free by a storm.

This wild day in March, in a little village far afield,
is a fitting day for the story that is to be told.

It is 1944, thirteen years since he passed from the
storms of this world that he loved, sixty-one years since
he came in through the door of birth. His life, in terms
of time, was a short life. But he neither lived nor
thought in terms of time. A word constantly upon his
lips was this: "We have eternity."

It was a word not idly spoken. It was his creed, and
it directed his life.

"The soul is mightier than space," he said, "stronger
than time, deeper than the sea, and higher than the
stars."

He was preoccupied during his entire life, with the

3

depths that he knew the spirit of man able to plumb and the heights that he was convinced man was destined to scale.

"Sin does not exist," he wrote, "except insofar as we have created it. It is we, therefore, who must destroy it. If we choose to make evil it exists until we do destroy it. Good we cannot make, for it is the very breath of the universe; but we can choose to breathe and live in it and with it."

This is Gibran. The West knows him as poet and painter, and as the author of *The Prophet*, that "little black book" of which the poet said, "While I was writing *The Prophet*, *The Prophet* was writing me."

The West knows him as a man with a vast spiritual vision and dream, a gentle person, loving and beloved, with a priceless sense of humour and a divine gift for friendship.

Here in the West is a small multitude of those who would say of him as Nietzsche said of Richard Wagner: "He realises all our desires; a rich, great, magnificent spirit, an energetic character, an enchanting man, worthy of all love, ardent for all wisdom . . . no one in the world knows him, no one can judge him, since the whole world builds on foundations that were not his, and is lost in his atmosphere. He is dominated by an idealism so absolute, a humanity so moving, that I feel in his presence as if I were in contact with divinity."

In the East they know the other Gibran, several of him. They know the man who was steel in velvet and

4

Gibran at Beirut in 1898

a sword in silk, the man whose bold poem *Spirits Rebel-lious* angered the Church, and stirred the Empire of the Turk, the Gibran who in his brief life created a definite literary style and originated a school of expression previously unknown to the Arabic tongue, and who has been for many years the pattern for young Arabic poets who call him their father and their Master.

In a slender volume of Arabic lyrics that came to his table one morning near the close of his life, was this inscription:

> To the resurrection of Eternal Poetry,
> To the spiritual flame which has awakened
> the Spirit of the East;
> To Gibran Kahlil Gibran, our Master,
> I dedicate my book,
> The echo of the echo of his voice.

Some there are who know the Gibran of the flashing mind, limitless in range and depth, the thinker who had come through the years to a profound and ordered scholarship; the man who once, for a jest, for a prank, dictated to three secretaries at one time, in three languages and on three different subjects — to the amazement of all concerned; the man whose springs of being were nourished ever from the soil of his nativity, Lebanon, for which he constantly dreamed a glorious future, and for which in his silence he devised systems of forestation and agriculture and the solution of economic and political problems.

5

"What Lebanon most needs," he said, "is one man with perhaps five or more millions of dollars, who will consciously and endlessly work for her growth and development, and for her realization of herself."

The Gibran who is least known to the world, both East and West, is the painter, the Gibran who has left an incredible and priceless legacy undreamed of by more than perhaps a few hundred souls on the planet. The drawings in the ten English books, significant and dominant as they are, are but an indication of the supreme bequest.

Gibran needed only a tag-end of paper and a stub of graphite to imprison in expression, with a few swift strokes both strong and delicate, some concept of essential beauty, even as with his brush and his colours upon a bit of canvas.

It may be said without fear of ultimate contradiction that when the verdict of the years is rendered this man will stand beside and not below the greatest masters of this graphic art by virtue of some divinely informed consciousness that we do not name. When his brush and his pencil visited canvas and paper, these became endued with a vital and vibrant force that rendered them no longer dead, but living.

Many persons ask, "Which did Gibran consider his greater art, which did he love best, his poetry or his painting?"

People asked him, and he smiled. And once he an-

6

swered the father of twin boys thus: "Which of your children can you say is nearer to your heart?"

The two gifts were with him from the beginning. When the little Kahlil was about four years old, he dug deep in the soil of the garden and planted small torn scraps of paper so that they might take root and grow into a tall bush that should produce fair white sheets for him to write and draw upon!

At six he was given a volume of Leonardo reproductions by his mother. After turning the pages for a few moments, he burst into wild weeping and ran from the room to be alone. His passion for Leonardo possessed him from that hour, so much so indeed, that when his father rebuked him for some childish misdemeanour the boy flew into a rage and shouted, "What have you to do with me? I am an Italian!"

He often said, "I do not see how they endured me. Only my mother, of all the world, could have understood that strange boy. I was a small volcano, a young earthquake."

And he told of a day when a great rain was falling, and it called to him, called his name, and he slipped off his little garments and ran out naked to answer the call of the rain, ran until his mother and his nurse, breathless, caught up with him and bore him struggling and protesting into the house.

His first poems were not written in words, but were modeled in snow and fashioned in stone. Figures of strange unchildlike beauty grew under his hands in his

7

father's garden all the long Winter, and the people would pass by and say, "See what the young Gibran has done now."

And when the Spring was come, the beautiful Nisan of the East, the snow melted and the anemone, "stained with the blood of Tammuz," blossomed in Lebanon, the child carried the stones and hewed them to build small churches and cathedrals under the shadows of the great dark trees.

Then, suddenly it seemed, he could write. Then there was but little modeling and building in him for awhile. Instead he wrote furiously, page after page, only to read and then tear the sheets into a thousand pieces. "It was never what I had wanted to say," was his explanation in telling of it.*

Soon, too, with coloured pencils and paints he was drawing and painting with a passion strange indeed for a young boy, and then destroying the pictures as soon as they were completed, because "they were never like what I saw when my eyes were dark."

This period of his early life was much in his mind when that life drew toward its close. He talked much of his mother, telling small incidents of such tender sweetness that both he and his listener would weep a little and then laugh because they had wept.

* This brings vividly to mind a day in 1929 when the studio in which K. G. had worked for fifteen years was undergoing a revolution of painting and furbishing, and he mused over hundreds of sketches and fragments of drawings, and then with calm deliberation destroyed scores of them, refusing to be dissuaded.

He told of the game he played with his mother. "My mother, Kamila Rahmi," he would say, and would tell of putting his little hands over his eyes and crying out, "You can't find Gibran! You can't see him!" "No," the mother would reply. "Where is my little Gibran? I have lost him." And he would fling up his arms and cry, "Here I am! Now, you can see me!"

The mother of this boy, Kamila Rahmi, was wise beyond the wisdom of many mothers. She knew almost in his infancy that the passion for freedom was in his blood, and he was restrained but little.

For hours he would sit brooding over the book of Leonardo, or gazing into the distance, or looking at the sun, for he had eyes that were never abashed before great light.

For hours he would remain perfectly quiet while his mother sang to him the soft wild plaintive songs of desert and mountain, in a voice of such enchanting beauty that "Kamila Rahmi's voice" is still a legend in the Lebanon; or while she read to him the tales of Haroun-al-Raschid or the hunting songs of Abu N'was.

Gibran said of his mother, "She lived countless poems and never wrote one." And he said also, "The song that lies silent in the heart of the mother will sing upon the lips of the child."

And it was true. While he lived his own countless poems, he sang also, both her songs and his own. And when she died, he said, "My life is shrouded, not because she was my mother, but because she was my friend."

9

It was perhaps the remembrance of his own childhood that prompted him to say and to believe that "every person is potentially an artist."

"A child may be taught to draw a bird as easily as to write the word. He may make rhymes while he is learning to make sentences, and he may model clay when he learns to build with his first blocks."

We have been playing around the outskirts of this thought in education, but we have not yet realized what such a consistent program might accomplish. We have forgotten — or have we? — that there is but one universal language and that its voice is art.

II

"DANGEROUS, REVOLUTIONARY, AND POISONOUS TO YOUTH"

There was a side of this many-sided being, Kahlil Gibran, that was like a child playing with life. I think I may say, in all truth, that there were but few who saw this puckish and enchanting aspect of the great man. It would show itself occasionally, in a flash, usually after long hours of creative work, when weary with the burden of his own genius he would throw it off like a garment. He would rise from his chair, or if he had been pacing the floor would turn suddenly and with an expression upon that changeful face that could be called nothing less than a grin, would say, "Now! I shall make for you a bit of modern American verse." This he would proceed to do — a stanza of doggerel, a ragged piece of absurd nonsense — but with a bite of humour that could outdo Ogden Nash or Samuel Hoffenstein at their impish best.

Then laughter, good, hearty, wholesome, healing laughter, until the tears would run down our cheeks. Always there followed a demand for a like production in return, and so contagious, so exhilarating, were his gayety and insistence that something ridiculous and witty managed to emerge.

Or perhaps it would be a bit of a dance, hand on hip and a pirouette, light and in imitation of a nimble-toed danseuse whose well-known theatrical smile he could mimic to perfection. Laughter again. And the weariness and burden were gone for the moment.

Also, behind the Gibran who wrote and spoke with authority and with full consciousness of his work and its worth was another one, a shy, reticent, almost shrinking person, again like a timid child, who said often, "Must I go and meet those new people? Must I stand up and speak before these others?" A painful high sensitivity that drew into itself, saying, "Must I answer the telephone?"

It was the reticence of a being thrust into an alien world, one whose mind and spirit never completely accepted and embraced the ways of Earth. He once said, "There are whole days at a time when I feel that I have just arrived from another planet. I am a man without yesterdays on this present Earth. Human contours are all strange to me, and human sounds."

He fully comprehended what he considered one of his limitations, saying, "I am not a good person. I should be wholly one with all that is upon this good Earth, but I cannot." He felt that he was failing in some measure to do all that was divinely expected of him. And in a bitter moment he once said, "I am a false alarm. I do not ring as true as I would."

12

The greatness of his vision and of his desire outran his human achievement. Yet his life was one uninterrupted ministration to those of his fellow beings who were in sorrow and in need. He was the most generous of souls, as certain of his countrymen, gifted but in untoward circumstances, can testify.

He was often imposed upon, and he knew that this was so, for no one ever fooled him for long, though persons who were a little stupid thought they had taken him in. He wrote: "A strange form of self-indulgence! There are times when I would be wronged and cheated, that I may laugh at the expense of those who think I do not know that I am being wronged and cheated."

I can remember a time when a mood of intense bitterness and pain was upon him. He told me something of the story. It concerned a real estate transaction in which he had allowed himself to become involved, and a very large sum of money was at stake. There were two women, and he said, "I must take these women to a court of law or lose this money. One of the women has come to me and has shaken the little black book [*The Prophet*] in my face, saying, 'You have written this book. Now what are you going to do about it?'" He was silent for a moment then he continued, "Can I go before a judge, believing what I believe and what I have written, and accuse these women? Can I sit in the witness chair and be questioned, to their condemnation?"

His face and voice were the answer to his question. He

13

could not, and I said just that, "You could never do it, being the self that you are."

His face cleared. "All of my friends tell me I must get the money. But if I should get it — so — I would never open the little black book again."

And then he wrote slowly on a bit of paper, "Let him who wipes his soiled hands on your garment take your garment. He may need it again; surely you would not."

Gibran once wrote, "Out of trouble and perplexity and happy anguish comes poetry that eases the heart." And it is this poetry, thus born, which has truly circled the Earth, having been translated into many languages, thereby ministering to the weary and the bewildered of the nations of the world.

In my own experience — and I am but one of many eternally grateful human beings constantly spreading his word — there has been a great body of evidence that the English books have come upon the mind and spirit of the multitudes with lightning power. I could fill a book with the record of expressions of joy and deep appreciation that have been spoken as well as written to me, and from the four corners of the Earth.

There was the little Fifth Avenue Bookshop with which I was closely identified for a time, in the Brevoort Hotel in New York City.

One afternoon there came down the steps and into the bright room a little old lady in gray. She had a sort of
14

wistful look on her face, but she smiled and looked around a little timidly.

"Can I help you?" I asked.

"Well — I don't know," she said, "but I hope so."

I waited.

"You see," she went on, "I want a book . . . and I don't know the name of it."

"Who wrote the book?"

"Well, I don't know that either." She looked a little bewildered.

"What kind of a book — poetry or a novel? Essays — biography?"

"I . . . I don't really know." Then she braced up and stated the case. "You see, a friend wrote me a letter and told me about the book. I've lost the letter, and I can't remember the name of the book or of the author. But there was something my friend quoted from the book. It said, 'Your pain is the breaking of the shell that encloses your understanding.'"

She repeated the line, as though it had become dear to her.

I went to the bookshelf, took down a copy of *The Prophet*, and turned to the chapter on *Pain*. I remember the look that swept across her sweet little old face. She took the book into her hand. She read the line, the page. She went and sat down in one of the comfortable needle-point chairs that were there for the very purpose of enticing our guests to sit down and stay. And she read,

15

entirely oblivious of me and of everything but what was before her on the page.

Others came, but still she took no notice. I do not know how long she sat there. But at length she came to me and said, "I want this book. Only . . . it isn't a book. It's bread and wine for tired people like me."

And there was a man interested in scientific research. He came to the studio during the 1932 exhibition, and this was his story. One day, a year or more before, he had been walking up Third Avenue, hurrying to keep an appointment. Passing by a small bookshop, he looked in at the window, a casual glance. There was a book standing against the background with the picture of a face on the jacket. He went on. As he went, the face in the picture somehow became clearer in his mind, gave him a strange feeling. He walked about three blocks, when suddenly he turned back. He had to look at that face again. He looked, and then went into the shop and bought the book. It was *The Prophet*.

Telling the incident, he said, "This book has opened to me the truth that science without the saving grace of beauty and compassion is a dead issue."

There was another man, a lawyer who sat through an hour of reading aloud from the same book in another bookshop in Philadelphia. He was a man full of years, with a benign countenance, and he listened with a quality of attention that could not fail to attract the reader's notice.

When the evening was over this lawyer came to speak

to me as others were doing, and he said, "I am a criminal lawyer. If I had read that chapter on *Crime* and *Punishment* twenty years ago I would have been a better and a happier man, and an infinitely better counsel for the defense."

Thus *The Prophet* brings to each individual soul its own peculiar fulfillment. The philosopher considers it philosophy; the poet calls it poetry. Youth has said of it, "Here are all the things that I have in my heart," and age has said, "All my days have I sought, knowing not what, and now in my Winter time I find my treasure in this book."

Whatever may have been in the consciousness of the man who set down the record of Almustafa, the chosen and the beloved, the consciousness of the sensitive reader will discover in it the expression of his own innermost mind and spirit.

The reason for this is fundamental. Gibran was not a theorist. He said, "If you must call me something, say I am a life-ist!" His words are not a clever arrangement of beautiful subtleties, but the simple and direct expression of man's greatest needs and of the answers to these needs.

How did he come by the answers? In the closing portion of his *Jesus, Son of Man*, the poet puts into the mouth of A Man from Lebanon Nineteen Centuries Afterward these words: "Seven times was I born, and seven times have I died. And now I live again. . . ." This may perhaps be the solution. For Gibran told us nothing new. There was and is nothing new to be told. His word is a restatement of essential truth that he had come through the ages to acquire. *The Prophet* is not a creation of Gibran's imagination, but rather a crystallization of accumulated love and wisdom. "Seven times have I lived . . . and now I live again."

Gibran was many things besides the poet who penned these stalwart and beautiful books and the painter who captured bits of eternity and placed them upon a sheet of paper. He was the psychologist with no taint of the psychoanalyst; the philosopher who had reduced his philosophy to the basic elements. He was the philologist who searched the golden history of words for very ecstasy, and not for scholarship. Yet he was also the profound scholar, seeking to conceal his vast learning, and forgetting as far as possible the intellectual achievements of the years.

He has been called an "audacious and daring soul," and so he was indeed. His audacity proceeded from beyond his human will and desire, and was in the nature of a great force that compelled him regardless of any personal consideration, for there was not an atom of aggressiveness in the man.

His boldness and daring became evident in his youth. His country, under the yoke of the Turkish Empire, was stricken in spirit, and hopelessness threaded all the fabric of its weaving. Gibran wrote a poem in his native Arabic, calling it *Spirits Rebellious*. It was published and circulated, and in an incredibly short time it was burned in the market place in Beirut by priestly zealots who pronounced it "dangerous, revolutionary, and poisonous to youth." The book was the first fist of the modern free youth to be shaken in the face of that powerful Empire, and it was shaken with unmistakable vigour.

Today the enterprising press agent would be on the scene. The young poet would be world news before midnight and the outrage would be discussed over the breakfast grapefruit the next morning.

But at the moment the incendiaries touched off this blaze, the author of this poisonous book, this dangerous and revolutionary youth of twenty, was a reticent soul working patiently at his painting in Paris, a pupil and friend of Rodin.

If he had been approached by the gentlemen of the press, which he was not, and if he had expressed himself to them he would have said — being interpreted in the vernacular of today — that the burning of *Spirits Rebellious* meant nothing in his young life. What he actually did say was this: "An excellent reason for immediately printing a second edition."

But the burning of the book was not the end. Gibran received in Paris information that for the writing of this poem he had been excommunicated from the Church and exiled from his country, for this unspeakable crime, a book calling upon the youth of his land for a realization of their high heritage and for a revival of the courage and the power and the glory of their forefathers, those men of ancient distinction and splendor, their Phoenician-Chaldean ancestors!

The edict of exile was remanded in 1908 when a new government became active in Turkey. And today in Beirut and in Antioch, in Cairo and in Alexandria, the little book that was burned has become a classic and is taught as such to the young students of Arabic literature.

III

"WE HAVE HARNESSED OUR EARTH"

The essential value of an artist's contribution to his audience is not, I believe, confined to what he pours into the work from his own consciousness, but it lies also in what that product of his love and work calls forth from the audience in consciousness and comprehension.

It has become increasingly evident to me that the level of consciousness prevailing among the hundreds of persons who have sought the opportunity to see and hear the work of Gibran wherever and whenever it has been presented is higher than I had anticipated. We hear much about the average human intelligence at this point in the world's progress — so called — being that of a twelve-year-old child. Well, perhaps the intelligence of said child is something to be considered. Having dealt with children in educational fields for many years, I have found that an average twelve-year-old boy or girl, other things being equal, will stand up rather well against the average person twice his or her age, and frequently put the elders to shame.

However, what I have found to be true is this: old or

young, dark skin or white, cultured or illiterate, Jew, gentile or pagan — I have seen not more than one half of one percent of those who came and saw and heard who were not touched in some depth of their nature, moved in some innermost of their being by what they saw and heard. This tells me that the contribution that Gibran has made to the art and literature of the world takes its place not only as such, but also as a powerful influence for the healing of the nations.

I have said many times, speaking to audiences large and small, and I say again: start with a community of fifty people who have the will and the tenacity to live out the conditions and the implications contained in the words of Almustafa, and we shall have the beginning of a millennium.

I hear frequently from students, young men and women in the universities of our country who are writing of Gibran for their major thesis. They ask to know more about him — himself. They are full of wonderings and questionings. It is a sign to me that his spiritual legacy has penetrated the consciousness of our young in a way that will yield its fruit in its season, a good rich harvest.

Over and over again they ask, "Do you think that Gibran is like William Blake in his work?"

I know that the opinion that Gibran is "the Blake of the twentieth century," attributed to Rodin, has been widely quoted, and intended as complimentary. I can think of no two artists more unlike in reality, aside from the bare facts that both were poets, painters and, of course, mystics.

Gibran painted man, the divine human, as a thing of sensitive beauty, flesh that is not fleshly, body that is disembodied of earthliness, spirit thinly veiled. Not so the English Blake. Gibran's subjects were never the saints and angels and demons of myth and legend, but were beings conceived in the dream of perfection, without fault or blemish.

In Blake, surely, we find an ecstasy, a rapture of abandon, the wild imaginings of a soul bemused by mystery. In Gibran the spirit motif is of an entirely different character. It is the poised revery of a soul wandering in dreams of infinity, but serene and harmonious, controlled, not violent. Both men were artists of vast vision, but there is a wide divergence between the paths they followed through the wilderness of human blindness and confusion. Each was his own man, and acutely individual.

Everywhere in Gibran's work there is evidence of his realization that man is nature and nature man. He recognizes one genesis, one law, one endlessness of love, and he says it continually in the simplest terms of line and colour.

There is a quality in many of these drawings that has been often commented on. In the remembrance of the faces there is a definite feeling of life and breath, the lift of an eyelid, the tremor of a lip, the rise of a breast in actual breathing, the blowing of a wind across a veiled

23

face. Having seen the drawings, one carries away, so one visitor to his studio said, "not the memory of pictures but of living souls."

I have said that Gibran knew full well the worth of his work. Many of the drawings have been left unsigned. When one or another of his friends would say, "Sign it, won't you?" He would laugh a little and say, "No! Why should I? It will still be known for a Gibran when I have lain long in the good dark earth beneath the cedars."

The good dark earth. The words were often upon his lips. He loved the actual soil and everything that grew from it. For trees he fostered a sense of reverence and worship, saying, "If there were but one tree in the world, the people of all nations would make pilgrimage to fall down and worship it."

He loved to touch natural wood. A piece of a broken branch picked up in a grove or forest he held and kept as a treasure, to carve, perhaps, into some lovely image. He cherished a collection of smallish stones, "brought from the shores of every sea upon the planet." He would finger them with more true pleasure than a hoarder of gold with his shining pieces.

His preoccupation with rock formation is everywhere apparent. The beautiful white figure of a woman, two fingers upon her lips, that is like an exquisite marble, shows a rocky background that on close scrutiny reveals the rocks to be closely knit figures of human beings. The picture is called *Silence*.

The oneness of man and nature, in rock, in cloud, in

24

tree, in stream and waterfall — all these are constantly emphasized in his work with pencil and brush. And his delight in one of these small masterpieces when it was complete and the reflection of the one in the other achieved was like that of a child who has found a treasure. It was strangely impersonal, as though he himself had had nothing to do with it.

Gibran, like all men of truly great genius, had no thought of his audience while he was creating. In fact, he was averse to the idea of having an audience save that of a relatively small circle of friends to whom he was devoted. In his maturer years he refused to allow his work to be exhibited, though efforts were made to persuade him. "No," he would say. "No. We will not show the drawings. They want to buy them!"

And buying and selling was not a part of his plan. He was taking a longer view, thinking of a world in which he foresaw conflict and terror and incredible disruption and desolation. He realized with all far-seeing men that the war through which the world had recently struggled had settled nothing, had certainly brought no peace.

He said, "It has been a war not for more freedom, but for more consciousness." And it is that "more consciousness" which is giving the nations today their undefeatable will to a victory that shall, this time, God willing, give to the world more freedom.

So this man from Lebanon was forging, in his own way, a weapon toward eventual peace. "Create Beauty," he said, "and let every other thing go to hell." And he

25

himself kept his own word to the letter, for he knew that the act of creating beauty throughout the world in the consciousness of the races of humanity and in their purpose and production would spell a great renascence of justice and compassion and worship. Thus would the good green Earth become a heavenly reality.

He had no illusion that this would come without long preceding agony and struggle and waiting. He knew better than most men that this century is but the dawn before the dawn. He knew, and he did not hesitate to say, that this monstrous misconception called progress must be stopped in its unholy tracks before the minds and spirits of men can once more be free to their rightful inheritance. "There is neither religion nor science beyond beauty," he said. And he raged with a burning indignation against the unspeakable stupidities that are committed in the name of religion and in the name of science.

"We have harnessed our Earth to the fiery steeds of science, and they are running away with our planet into a hell of machinery," he wrote only a short time before his death.

During the late war Gibran had conceived a bitter and deep-seated aversion to the vision that had come to him of what the conquest of the air would do to the world and the nations of the world. He once said, "If I could I would destroy every airplane upon the Earth, and every remembrance of that flying evil from men's minds."

Someone asked him, "Why should you say such a terrible thing?" And he replied furiously, "Because man is not a being of the air. He has been put upon the Earth. The Earth is his home and his kingdom, and he is not yet master of that kingdom. All the angels and archangels and all the hosts of the above-world will take their vengeance upon man if he does not abandon his unholy disturbance of their free ether. Let only the wingéd spirit of man fly unto the invisible height."

It was a subject that he could not discuss without indignation and grief. He said, "Destruction and desolation shall visit all the lands of the Earth, and the young men and the maidens shall go down in their path like buds stripped from the almond and the olive trees, and no fruit therefrom."

He predicted the fall of cities, and referred once to the words in *The Prophet* where it is written, "In their fear your forefathers have gathered you too near together. And that fear shall endure a little longer. A little longer shall your city walls separate your hearths from your fields."

"And then," he said, "a day will dawn, a new day — the time will come when we shall return again, and it will not be so. The Earth will be the Lord's, and the fulness thereof."

There was another vision, a dream that he dreamed. He said, "I would build a city near to a harbor, and upon an island in that harbor I would erect a statue, not to Liberty but to Beauty. For Liberty is that one about whose feet men have forever fought their battles; and Beauty is that one before whose face all men reach hands unto all men as brothers."

Gibran was overconscious of the mental and spiritual, as well as the physical, poverty of a large proportion of the world's people. He knew their blindness. Over and over he has drawn and painted *The Blind*, and he meant not the blind-eyed, but the blind-hearted.

The sorrows and the stumblings of humanity — these engrossed him wholly with a burning passion. And he knew them well, for he had ample reason to know.

The years in the studio were a succession of endless ministrations to human trouble and woe. Day after day, those who were in perplexity or anguish climbed the long flights of stairs and handed over their burdens to this man from another country, another world, and, it seemed often, from another time. His quick comprehension was never-failing, neither was his almost instant finding of some way to solve the problem, or at the least to renew the courage and endurance, of the troubled one. It was simply done — a quiet reminder of some timeless truth, some law of life, which from his lips had nothing of dogma or doctrine, but came as healing for the unseen wound.

If there be one word by which to characterize this man complete, entire, both himself and his work, the rock of his foundation, the cornerstone of his building, that word will be simplicity. The same word applies to

28

a few other of the Titans of the ages, of whom Gibran wrote saying, "Socrates, Jesus, Jeanne d'Arc and Lincoln — the four most beautiful beings the world has ever known, put to death! And there was laughter upon the lips of the sky!"

He practiced this same simplicity in his everyday living and doing. During a period of his life when he was entertained, dining out frequently, and being feasted as his friends were overjoyed to feast him, he would give himself "a spot of fasting" as he said, "to overcome what they, in their affection, have done to me!"

He liked a frugal supper in the studio, and he liked making a game of it. This was another of his ways of putting off, for a time, the weight of his endowment. He would say, "In the East there is a custom of eating all from one huge vessel. Let us have our soup tonight in one bowl!"

So we would arrange the small table with one large bowl of soup. There were always croutons, many croutons, and the soup was thick, a puree. We would be seated with ceremony. Then, taking the soup spoon, Gibran would draw an imaginary line through the middle of the soup, saying with the greatest gravity, "This is your half of the soup, and your half of the croutons, and this other is my half. See to it that we neither one trespass upon the soup and the croutons of the other!"

Then laughter and a thorough enjoyment, each of his own half of the soup! Next a glass of wine and breadsticks to be dipped in the wine — another of his favourite

29

pleasures. Then the cigarette. And one would never have guessed, seeing it all, that the man who played the game so heartily and with such merriment in his laughter was the same who said of himself, "What a pity that men will not weave for me a garland until the day when my head shall be so high beyond their reach that they cannot place it above my head."

He deplored the complications and complexities of modern living. He wanted so passionately to retain the ancient beautiful things and to reconcile them with the lives of today's sons and daughters, but he wanted it to come about simply and naturally. He said, "Life and love and death are the great facts of existence, be it East or West." And he saw that these three importances were subordinated to every sort of artificial nonsense.

"Symbolism!" he exploded one day. "Take away the word. Let us say 'truth made visible,' if you like, tangible beauty. Simplicity, not symbolism."

Simplicity—that divine quality for lack of which the world of human beings is lost and wandering in time and space.

IV

"THE MAGIC OF THE ARABIC"

It has been my privilege to know many of the most distinguished of our Lebanese-American citizens, and to realize the depth and height of the love and pride they cherish for this poet who was their countryman. Gibran spent all except two of the first twenty years of his life on that soil from which the great prophets and seers of old had sprung. Even during those early years he had, through the beauty and the courage of his life and utterance, enshrined himself in the hearts of the hundred and fifty million students and scholars and lovers of beauty who read the Arabic language, and to as many more who speak the tongue, though they perhaps neither read nor write it.

It seemed incredible to me when I learned that there are upon the face of the Earth three hundred million Arabic-speaking people, but such is the fact.

There is a story told of an American lady who was traveling in Lebanon, and meeting a young Lebanese poet, said to him, "I know a countryman of yours in New York — Kahlil Gibran. Do you know of him?" And the young poet replied, "Madame, do I ask you if you know of Shakespeare?"

31

Gibran's Arabic work bulks large in the total of his writing output. There are numerous volumes, the first one having been a small book on *Music*, which immediately attracted the attention of the Arabic art world. There are the volumes called *The Book of Tears and Laughter, Tempests, Nymphs of the Valley*, and *Broken Wings*, besides *Spirits Rebellious*, the most dynamic and most widely known of them all, and one compilation entitled *Al Badayih wal Tarayiff*, meaning *Beautiful and Rare Sayings* — this last culled from Gibran's wealth of Arabic essays and poems and articles contributed to the leading Arabic magazines and press.

This last mentioned book contains reproductions of drawings made by Gibran at the age of seventeen, pen-and-ink sketches of seven or eight pre-Islamic poets. Of these sketches the artist said, "There were no pictures of these great men, so my imagination helped me to draw their faces." The drawing of Avicinna strongly resembles Leonardo da Vinci. "He *was* like da Vinci," Gibran declared.

When the book, really an anthology, was published, Gibran was astonished. "I had forgotten all about the drawings," he said. "I do not know where they have been hiding, nor how the publisher got hold of them."

During his whole life he was prodigally generous with permissions for the use of his poems and pictures in reproduction. *The Prophet*, translated into almost two score languages, yielded him, he once said, " the sum of twenty-four dollars from the firm in Holland that published the Dutch *Prophet*. I never ask them for royalties," he added, as though that were a matter of course.

At St. Mark's In-the-Bouwerie, New York, one of the city's oldest churches, an adaptation of *The Prophet* is given every year as a religious drama. It was there, as aforesaid, that the book was first read to the public, shortly after its publication. The same church has a vesper service at which the entire office is "drawn from the rhythms of Kahlil Gibran, poet-prophet of Lebanon." The chanting of these majestic themes to superb organ music, once heard, is never to be forgotten. These several observances were initiated by Dr. William Norman Guthrie, who entertained a profound faith in the mission of Gibran as a modern prophet. And it was Dr. Guthrie, also, who referred to the book *Jesus, The Son of Man*, as "The Gospel according to Gibran."

In form these "rhythms" — the poetry of Gibran — are comparable to nothing so nearly as to the King James version of the English Bible. The same clarity of expression, the same simplicity, the same power of enchantment are here, and his phrase and his imagery derive, naturally, from the same ancestry.

The fine legacy of Arabic poetry which he has left is still a hidden treasure to the English speaking world. It will demand no one less than a great English poet who has mastered the intricacies and the nuances of the Arabic to bring "the magic of the Arabic into the magic of the English." It will never be merely a matter of correct translation, but always one of passionate re-crea-

33

tion into Gibran's adopted language from his native tongue.

Shortly after Gibran took up his residence in New York City, there was organized in his studio the Arabic Academy. I have found among some notes jotted on a small paper these words: "Our Academy is composed of twelve Syrian poets, most of them young, and there will be no more than twelve. Only death will make place for a new poet to find a place in this circle. The Academy is the mother of the ones in Aleppo, Cairo, Damascus, Beirut and Tripoli."

Among these twelve the finest traditions of the great Arabic poetry were to be "nurtured with a three-fold passion, faith and love and work, to the end that the seeds of beauty and truth that were from the beginning shall live and blossom in the literature of the Arabic people and in their heart."

In the years that have passed since that time the leader of the Academy, Kahlil Gibran, and three others of these poets have died. One, who shall be nameless, has departed from the faith. The others continue with the same devotion and loyalty to their noble inheritance and to the memory of their beloved friend and country-man who has preceded them unto the above-world.

Let us not, however, imagine for one moment that the loyalty of these men to Gibran has been a matter wholly of kinship or of sentiment, for they are, each and every one, men of gifts and the highest integrity who early recognized what manner of man was in their midst, and

Gibran at 25, from an oil by Yusef Hoyiek

who with one accord looked to him as to one of greater power and vaster wisdom, one informed from some mystic Source that they knew not. Yet they met together with pleasure and joyous discourse, reading their poems and listening to the poems of their friends, discussing, arguing, sometimes having a "grand fight" as Gibran put it, for they are men of force, and none to be thrown from his position without cause.

I have heard Gibran speak hundreds of times of "my Academy." Its members were his spiritual kin, as well as men from the same earthly country. They spoke his language, not only the Arabic of their native tongue, but the language of his deepest heart, the language of the poet, of beauty and truth, and of things ancient and beautiful, honor and justice and compassion.

And here they were, in the midst of the hectic America of the early twentieth century, making a mighty stand for all the good things in which they believed. It is no wonder that Gibran said "my Academy," with only a little less fervor than he said "my country."

Gibran had great faith in what the thousands of Lebanese and Syrians who are now American citizens might contribute to the development of our national life, and to our art and literature.

Even to the very end of his life he continued writing in his well-beloved native tongue. And more and more as the months passed he liked to read aloud from the Arabic, for the sheer pleasure of hearing the sound of the words. It was one of his pleasures to take his Arabic

Bible and read from it, from the Book of Ruth, or Isaiah, or the lesser prophets, translating each verse as he went, so that we might compare this translation with the English version. It is one of my few regrets in connection with our work together that I did not at those times, take down his beautiful translation from the Arabic, for there were subtle and sometimes breath-taking divergences that I would wish to have preserved.

His rendering of the words of Jesus was of very particular interest, for he was familiar with every nuance of the Aramaic that Jesus spoke, and his translation made it evident that the English Bible has in many instances departed from the original intention of the words spoken by the young Nazarene. These basic differences were strongly in his mind during the writing of his book, *Jesus, The Son of Man.*

Many times during the making of that book the poet broke into a flood of Arabic, in a passion because there was not an English word that conveyed with perfect exactitude the meaning of the thought he wanted to express, there being, as he said, "fifty words in Arabic to give expression to the many aspects of love," while in English there is but one. His vast Arabic vocabulary made him feel cramped in his adopted tongue. However, that very fact resulted in the pure and almost perfect clarity and simplicity of his English style.

When the book *Jesus* was published in 1928, a comment in the *Springfield Union* said, "Gibran's English is marked by its beauty and its clarity. It attains a degree of perfection that might well serve as an inspiration for other writers to whom English is their native tongue."

And I make no doubt that it has so served.

It was about this time that the *Manchester Guardian*, discussing contemporary writers of eminence, included in the essay the names of six men whom they considered distinguished above all others for the excellence of their English achievements; among them, curiously enough, were two writers not born to the language, Kahlil Gibran and Joseph Conrad.

And at the same period Claude Bragdon expressed himself thus: "The character and depth of his influence upon the entire Arabic world may be inferred from the fact that it gave rise to a new word, *Gibranism.* Just what this word means English readers will have no difficulty in divining: mystical vision, metrical beauty, a simple and fresh approach to the 'problems' of life . . . extraordinary dramatic power, deep erudition, lightning-like intuition, lyrical life, metrical mastery, and Beauty which permeates the entire pattern in everything he touches."

And all this springing from a source that impelled the poet to pronounce himself in this one mighty sentence: "Work is love made visible."

To the conformist and the hide-bound Gibran was

unpredictable. He was once asked for fundamental rules and laws for a consistent and ordered life.

"I lay down no rules of conduct," was the reply. "Do whatsoever you will so long as you do it beautifully."

The whole fabric of his thinking and living was so simple and direct that it baffled the man and the woman who were investigating intricate and complicated systems of ethics, philosophies, and isms.

"Religion?" in answer to a query. "What is it? I know only life. Life means the field, the vineyard and the loom. . . . The Church is within you. You yourself are your priest."

And again on the same subject: "Religion among men is but a field tilled by those who have a purpose; some hopeful for the bliss of eternity, some ignorant, fearful of future flame."

And still again: "All that is worth while is a free spirit. And this means as many different things as there are different human beings."

It was inevitable that this "outrageous" attitude toward orthodoxy should arouse heated and furious opposition, which it did. There were repeated attacks upon his position, all of which disturbed him not at all.

One of the loudest dissenters to his views once said to him, "What are you trying to do? Get up a new cult?"

Gibran's eyes glowed, and a ring came into his voice as he replied, "My friend" — some slight suspicion of a gentle irony in his words — "I shall carve a stone and place it in a field, the cornerstone for a new Temple.

38

Then I shall die, having done all that I, in my simplicity am able to do. But mark you, long after my death another shall come and add another stone. So, countless generations shall be born and die, and in each generation a brother of mine shall hew a stone and build it, until the Temple is completed. And the Temple shall be the dwelling-place for the Most High."

Organized religion had no attraction for this man. He would not argue the subject. When some ardent cultist would seek to convince him of the supervalue of a particular creed or dogma, the poet would answer, "Yes, it is all on the way." And he would quote afterward, the old Upanishad maxim, "Never argue with the once-born."

He wrote in that book of priceless sayings, *Sand and Foam:* "Once in every hundred years Jesus of Nazareth meets Jesus of the Christian in a garden among the hills of Lebanon. And they talk long; and each time Jesus of Nazareth goes away saying to Jesus of the Christian, 'My friend, I am afraid we shall never, never agree.'"

When his last breath was spent there was consternation among his people. Gibran, their "Habibi" — Beloved — had not responded to the Maronite priest who had ardently sought to arouse him in his last hour to a consciousness of the rites he wished to administer.

Gibran, their great poet, their countryman, richly endowed with rare genius, had given little or no attention to the rituals and observances of the Church. There were those who questioned his right to a place in the assemblage of the faithful dead, but not for long. Love and faith and a great national pride conquered the littleness of sectarianism. And every gesture within the gift of the Maronite Church, into which Gibran was born, was lavishly accorded to this man from Lebanon after his death.

In this connection I wish to quote from the pen of a countryman and a close friend of Gibran's, Salloum A. Mokarzel, a distinguished Lebanese editor and writer, one of the leaders of the thousands of Lebanese and Syrian Americans in the United States, and a communicant of the Maronite Church.

He wrote in *The Syrian World*, a magazine which was for years the heartbeat of these devoted citizens of our country: "It does seem incongruous to many that the man whose iconoclastic tirades against conventional sectarianism (which would limit and monopolize the grace of God to an initiated few) aroused the animosity of some religious officials in high places, should finally receive the obsequies and approved rites of a sectarian Church. But in truth there is nothing incongruous about it. Like all great mystics Gibran was intensely religious. And it was because he was intensely religious that he rebelled against all bounds and limitations which would estrange the soul from its legitimate and free share of participation of the divine.

"The same wrath that burned in Jesus, who drove the traders and money-changers from the Temple, burned in Gibran who, in one of his parables in *The Wanderer*, makes a lightning fall on the head of a bishop who repulsed a non-Christian woman who had come to him asking if there be salvation for her from hell-fire.

"And as Jesus justified the poor tax-gatherer who humbly confessed his sins before God, so also Gibran counted among the saved many millions of all races, languages and creeds who had never been baptized by water and the Spirit.

"Hundreds of years before him the great Arab mystical poet, Ibn Al-Farid, of whose *Taiyyah* Gibran was so fond, had sung:

And if to a stone a Buddha worshiper doth bow,
His fellowship in faith I still forsooth avow.

"And with an equal majestic sweep of universal love also, Ibn Al-Arabi, perhaps the greatest Arab mystic of all time, also sang:

My heart is capable of every form;
A cloister for the monk, a fane for idols;
A pasture for gazelles, the votary's Kaaba;
The tables of the Torah, The Koran.
Love is the faith I hold, wherever turn
His camels, still the one true faith is mine."

It was with the power and authority of such traditions that Gibran took his place in the procession traveling from "ex-eternity to eternity."

Now Gibran, to use our mortal word, is dead. But he said, "If I die, I shall not go far from this good green

41

Earth, not for a long, long time." And indeed, there has never been in the hearts of those who knew him best any feeling of lostness or inconsolable grief. His vast and loving spirit lives in every word of his words, and we feel and know that it is so. Something of him will remain throughout the years and the ages, under the shade cast by the Cedars of the Lord. His bone and brain and brawn will, at last, pass into the good dark Earth, into the tough roots, and up to the great branches overhead.

All that was Earth in him — it is his own fine phrase — shall know perpetual resurrection and beauty through the seasons, rains, and snows, and through the tumults of all winds and tempests that he loved.

The atoms of his dust shall live and die a thousand thousand times in Lebanon. And ten thousand times ten thousand pilgrims shall kneel upon that sod and call him blessed.

V

"WHY AM I HERE?"

The first of the "little black books" to appear in English was *The Madman* published in 1918 by Alfred A.
Knopf, head of one of the younger publishing houses,
a man with an unerring instinctive sense of literary
values.

This volume is in part translation from the Arabic
parables, in part written directly in English. A small
book of only seventy pages, it is a product of the poet's
youth and early manhood, rich with promise of what
was to follow. It is entirely of the East, with no shading
of Western thought or content. It is an expression of the
passionate inner life not yet restrained and controlled by
the vaster wisdom and compassion that came to bud in
The Forerunner and to full flower in *The Prophet*.

We find in *The Madman* parables a fine irony, and
also certain intimations of disillusion and a sharp bitterness against life. Witness the closing piece from which
we take these lines:

God of lost souls, thou who art lost amongst the
gods, hear me: . . .

I dwell in the midst of a perfect race, I the most
imperfect.

> I, a human chaos, a nebula of confused elements,
> I move amongst finished worlds — peoples of com-
> plete laws and pure order. . . .
>
> To rob a neighbor with a smile . . . to praise pru-
> dently, to blame cautiously, to destroy a soul with a
> word, to burn a body with a breath, and then to wash
> the hands when the day's work is done. . . .
>
> Why am I here, O God of lost souls . . . ?

Yet it is here also that we find that sublime utterance, that revelation of timeless memory which says:

> And after a thousand years I climbed the sacred
> mountain and again spoke unto God, saying, "My
> God, my aim and my fulfillment; I am thy yesterday
> and thou art my tomorrow. I am thy root in the earth
> and thou art my flower in the sky, and together we
> grow before the face of the sun."

And we have here the young poet crying out through the Madman, his masks having been stolen, "Blessed, blessed are the thieves who stole my masks," and rejoicing because thus he had "found both freedom and safety in my madness; the freedom of loneliness and the safety from being understood, for those who understand us enslave something in us."

These parables show him in rebellion against hypocrisy and blindness and stupidity. The conflict in his Self, his Seven Selves of which he writes, is still going on.

Here for the first time Gibran registers fully his sense of that aloneness which remained with him always, even unto the end. Always he was alien to this planet, to this time and this scene, yet always he battled to reduce the distance between himself and ourselves. But as he once said, "Ye would not."

The words I have previously quoted from Nietzsche concerning Wagner are literally true of Gibran: "The whole world builds on foundations which are not his, and is lost in his atmosphere." And there were times when the realization of this terrible aloneness over-whelmed him with heartbreaking assault. And no sur-cease this side of eternity.

"Why am I here, O God of lost souls, thou who art lost amongst the gods?"

Almost immediately after the publication of *The Madman* the book went into French, German, Italian and Spanish translations and became widely known and prized in the Latin countries and in South America, where there are thousands of Arabic-speaking people who honour Gibran's name and every word and work of his.

Gibran had many delightful memories of this period of his life. He acquired the friendship of the younger American writers, his contemporaries, and enjoyed a companionship that was a mutual joy and enrichment. He infused into their spirit an essence as old as time, and they opened to him the depth and beauty of the real poets in this Western world.

The reception given to *The Madman* being reason enough, it was followed in 1920 by *The Forerunner*,

45

again in part translation from his Arabic, but a book of
wider vision, deeper wisdom, and a warm and tender
compassion, still with a touch of controlled irony, still
seeing behind the veil of illusion, yet without the shading of bitterness and with a surge of love and yearning.

Herein we find the superb poem entitled *Love* with
its few lines, almost in words of one syllable, and the
starkest and most beautiful confession of yearning:

> They say the jackal and the mole
> Drink from the self-same stream
> Where the lion comes to drink.
>
> And they say the eagle and the vulture
> Dig their beaks into the same carcass,
> And are at peace, one with the other
> In the presence of the dead thing.
>
> O Love, whose lordly hand
> Has bridled my desires,
> And raised my hunger and my thirst
> To dignity and pride,
> Let not the strong in me and the constant
> Eat the bread or drink the wine
> That tempt my weaker self.
> Let me rather starve,
> And let my heart parch with thirst,
> And let me die and perish,
> Ere I stretch my hand

To a cup you did not fill,
Or a bowl you did not bless.

The Last Watch, the piece with which the volume
closes, reveals a vast understanding released in the poet's
being, putting away all lesser emotion and comprehension. It is a fitting precursor to *The Prophet*, which
followed three years later.

The Forerunner gathered friends and admirers for
the man from Lebanon by leaps and bounds, and the inevitable translations followed.

In my many readings from the books I have found
several of the parables in *The Forerunner* to be known
and requested time and again. Among these *Said a
Sheet of Snow-white Paper*, *The Scholar and the Poet*,
Out of My Deeper Heart, and *God's Fool* seem to be
of greatest interest. The last mentioned is one of the
most touching and beautiful tales among all the parables.

This form of story peculiar to the East, so ancient and
yet so telling, was Gibran's chosen method of driving
home a truth. The form is as unfailing as it is unique.
I know of no contemporary who is able to use this technique with such certain deftness. It is a challenge to any
modern writer.

I myself took a fling at it during Gibran's later years,
for it had always intrigued me. There was a pleasant
argument when he said, "You could write a parable if
you should wish to." I insisted that I could not. He faced
me with a boyish grin and shouted, "Well, I dare you!"

47

This always worked, and he knew it. So I set out to make the attempt.

Then there came to my mind a story that Gibran had related of an occurrence one night when he was going back to the studio from a dinner and his taxi broke down. He started to walk home, and was met by a man whom he guessed to be a sailor, probably out of a berth. The man accosted him, asking for money for a drink. From this point of departure I was on my way, with the following result:

The Prince and the Seafarer

It was night upon the King's Highway.

In the royal chariot the Prince came riding to the Palace from a great banquet which had been set to do him honor. Passing through a thick grove, at the edge of it, the wheel of the chariot struck upon a huge rock and suffered hurt.

The charioteer alighted from his chariot, and seeing that it was become unsafe to bear the sacred person of the Prince, he fell upon his knees and besought him, saying, "Great and Imperial Majesty, what shall now become of me, seeing that I have thus wrought this mischance upon you?"

And the Prince was a true Prince, and he answered and said, "God lives. And He is the maker of night, and of the stones in His groves by the wayside. Fear not. See, the Palace is but a good stone's throw away. In the cool and under the stars I shall walk to my

Father's house, and no harm shall come to me, or thee."

And he did so, carrying in his heart the words of blessing from the lips of the charioteer who loved him.

And the way of the Prince lay through the public square. And he looked upon his people, and they looked carelessly upon him, and knew not that he was their Prince.

And as he approached the Inn of the city, one accosted him, asking alms. And the Prince saw that he was a seafaring man, and he paused to listen both because he was the Prince, and because his own soul yearned ever for the sea.

And the Prince said, "I perceive that you are a seafarer and no beggar. What would you with my alms?"

And the stranger laughed with bitter laughter and replied, "Ay, you say truly. A seafaring man am I, with no ship and no port, and between four walls I must lie down to sleep. And there is a taste of death in my mouth. And I ask alms that I may go into yonder Inn and drink wine unto forgetfulness."

And the Prince was of great compassion, for he was also a seafarer who must needs lie between four walls for his kingdom's sake, and he knew the taste of the bitterness that was like unto death.

And he said, "What shall be the measure of the gold you require for the fulfillment of your wish?"

And the stranger said bitterly, "Much gold."

And the Prince said, "How much?"

And the seafarer looked into his face unbelieving, and answered wildly, "Three hundred piastres!"

And the Prince opened his scrip of gold and took therefrom such an amount, and offered it to the stranger.

"Take it, friend, and go and drink wine unto forgetfulness. But one thing I ask: that when you are well-nigh come unto the moment of forgetting, you will arise and go unto your own four walls. I would not have you thrown into the street when the Inn shall be closed and become dark and silent."

For the night grew cold and the Prince perceived that the seafarer had left his cloak at home.

And the seafaring man said, "You offer me three hundred piastres to go unto the Inn and make myself drunken?"

And the Prince said, "Is not that your desire?"

Then there was silence for a space.

And the seafaring man said, "I desire only a bowl of lentils. Give me, if you will, three piastres."

But the Prince pressed upon him saying, "Nay, take these, and do with them as you will, wine or lentils. They are yours and welcome."

But he would not.

And even unto the door of the Inn the Prince accompanied the seafarer. But the King's son could not prevail upon him.

And the seafarer took three piastres and entered

50

the Inn, and the Prince went unto the royal Palace.

And for the seafarer and for the Prince there is no wine of forgetfulness.

This was my parable which was later published in *The New Orient*. The conclusion of the actual incident was thus: the man on Sixth Avenue, when Gibran had asked how much he required to become drunken, had said, "A dollar!" But when the dollar was held out to him, something had come to life within his consciousness, and he refused it saying, "No. Give me ten cents for a cup of coffee."

When we read the tale together, Gibran, in his generosity said, "You see! I have told you that you are Lebanese!"

This was an allusion to a game we played sometimes to lighten the strain of too great exaltation of spirit. One of the long silken garments, the ivory and gold one, about my shoulders, and a veil upon my head, and I became "the Lebanese." He would say, "Any moment I expect you to break out into Arabic." It was childlike; it made him happy — and it gave me the thrill of something half-forgotten and yet half-remembered, Lebanon — the mountains and the Cedars. And curiously enough when I found myself actually in that land some years later, going up those indescribably glorious mountains, going to Bsherri, to the Cedars, none of it was strange to me. It was as though the modern world had dropped away. I was back, far back in some medieval time, and

51

very much at home, with a great peace and sense of fulfillment flowing over me. The people, with their poetry
and beauty and their almost embarrassing hospitality —
they were not of today, but they were not strange to me.
I was one of them.

But that, as we say, is another story.

VI

"TRUTH IS HERE"

The Forerunner concluded with these words:

But suddenly he raised his head, and like one waking from sleep he outstretched his arms and said, "Night is over, and we children of night must die when dawn comes leaping upon the hills; and out of our ashes a mightier love shall rise. And it shall laugh in the sun, and it shall be deathless."

And in three years came *The Prophet*, that witness of "the mightier love" to "laugh in the sun." And it is the belief of thousands who know the book that it will indeed "be deathless."

The book was conceived during the poet's fifteenth year while he was a student at the Madrasat Al-Hikmat, The School of Wisdom — now the College de la Sagesse — in Beirut.

Kahlil Gibran had been but eleven years of age when he made the journey to America, to Boston, with his mother, his half-brother Peter, and his younger sisters, Marianna and Sultana.

When the boy was in his fourteenth year he insisted violently on returning to his own country to complete his education in the Arabic world of literature and culture. In the early Autumn of that year he took ship alone and went back to the land of his nativity. He did not go as a gay youth leaving for an exhilarating adventure in the student life, but rather as a young soul who had always been old, who had a burden upon his heart, whose mind dwelt more upon death than upon life, who knew himself to be the alien, the outsider, and who had yet to learn the definite direction and the full extent of his powers.

He talked once, I think only once, of that voyage to Beirut. I shall never forget that once.

"I was in a dream," he said. "It was not a clear or a pleasant dream. It was confused and uncertain. My mother, my brother Peter, my two sisters — there in Boston. My mother — she who lived countless poems and never wrote one. . . . My father — in the mountains of Lebanon, close to the Cedars. . . . I — this young thing, daring to set my will against all their wills. But I knew — *I knew* that I could only be what I had it in me to be if I went back to my country. It was in me to be a poet and a painter!" He stopped and pounded on the table with his fist, a fist that was like iron. Then he rose and stood. "And I am a poet and a painter! I am a good poet and a good painter, and I like my poems and my paintings! I shall shout it in the street if I feel like doing it!"

He was shouting there in the studio, like a boy asserting his prowess in some favorite sport.

54

Suddenly he smiled, a strange kind of smile that made my eyes misty.

"Am I a vain peacock?" he asked. "Or do you also like my poems and my paintings?"

But before I could answer — "Sh!" he said, two fingers upon his lips, "I know." And he began pacing up and down.

"Well . . . when I reached Beirut and went to the College to enter for my schooling, they asked me, 'Who has brought you here? Who is with you in this?' I straightened myself — I was not very high, you know — and I said, 'Sir, no one has brought me here. I am with myself.' Of course they knew — they had the letters. . . . And then everything cleared in my mind. There were no more clouds. My spirit was no longer confused. I was with my Self — and that was enough."

Here, then, two years later he wrote the first version of *The Prophet,* and having written put it aside, knowing, he said, that it was "a green fruit," knowing that a time would come when he should take it out again and that it would be a power in his hand.

"That *being,*" he said, [Almustafa] "has always been with me, I think."

It has seemed to me and to many others that Almustafa was Gibran's self, that if you would have the autobiography of his spirit you may read it in *The Prophet* and in *The Garden of the Prophet,* which came some time later.

Another three years, and his college life concluded with the highest honours, he went to Paris to embark upon the great adventure of his painting life. The story of that period is one of devotion to a changeless purpose: work, work, and more work. We might relate incidents that occurred, friendships that he formed, all of which had their effect upon the future of this man's life, but on the whole he was living within himself, strengthening his forces against the coming years, not knowing, yet with a sense of foreboding, how full of struggle and pain those years were to be.

The history of *The Prophet* from the moment of its beginning is, I believe, unparalleled. Gibran carried it with him when he went to Paris, and thence to Boston when he was summoned, a youth of twenty, to his mother's bedside. And he read to her what he had written of the young Almustafa.

The mother, wise in her son's youth as she had been in his childhood, said, "It is good work, Gibran. But the time is not yet. Put it away."

He obeyed her to the letter. "She knew," he said, "far better than I, in my green youth."

At twenty-five, again in Paris, the now widely known young painter, who had attracted the notice and friendship of Rodin, and whose paintings were twice hung in the *Salon*, rewrote the entire poem, still in Arabic. Reading it aloud to himself, who had now no living mother to counsel him, he said, "It is good work, Gibran. But the time is not yet — not yet. Put it away!"

And once more the tale of Almustafa, the chosen and the beloved, was put away until another ten years had passed.

For two of these intervening years Gibran remained in Paris — more work, more study, more friendships. He met and made drawings of some of the most distinguished men in the world of art at that time; Henri Rochefort, Debussy, Maeterlinck, Edmond Rostand, the younger Garibaldi, and Rodin.

Soon after his return to America, Gibran took up his residence in New York City, feeling that here in the heart of the Western world he would find a way to translate his desire to create truth and beauty and the essence of the true art of living into words and pictures. He wanted the artist's life, and he chose the old Studio Building at 51 West Tenth Street, the first building ever erected in the United States for the express and exclusive use of artists and sculptors. These surroundings seemed to lend themselves to his desire for solitude and freedom for his work.

It was there that he formed a close friendship with Albert Ryder, like himself a solitary and, also like himself, bearing a burden of sorrow upon his soul, not wholly understood.

And all this time this man from Lebanon, one of the company of the immortals who visit this planet once in a thousand years with a message from the Most High, was making ready to deliver that message through the singing words of the poet and the line and form and colour of the painter.

Here then, the first English *Prophet* was written. It was the beginning of the message. *The Madman* and *The Forerunner* had been but the preparation, the foreshadowing of the delivery. They had been the trickling of mountain streams from their source in the depths of the soil of this man's Earth-being. *The Prophet* was the river.

It was written again, not translated from the Arabic, but composed and set down directly in English. Pacing up and down the length of the studio, stopping to write upon the page, pacing again, walking in the white nights of our northern Winter through Central Park, walking through the Cohasset woods near the sea during the Summer season, he transformed the magic of the Gibran Arabic into the magic of the Gibran English. And this amazing book was rewritten by the poet's own hand five times over a period of five years before it was given to the printed page.

The actual writing of his English poems was always a difficult task for the poet. When he could pace, thinking in Arabic, and speaking the English translation without the interruption of going to his table to put down the words, he was happiest in his creation.

He once said, "It took me five years to write the English *Prophet*. With you I would have done it in one year."

The writing was done in brown notebooks, always brown notebooks.

Gibran wrote once: "Would that someone could make up my mind for me in all things of everyday life. I am so busy about *One Thing* that I have no time to choose between this and that." And yet he often exhibited the most whimsical and delightful persistence concerning the smallest details.

He had used since childhood these same brown books, like a schoolboy's composition books. He said, "We know what *they* do not know — that poems can be written only in brown books!" and laughed at himself for saying so.

It was his habit, when the newest brown book was brought to his table, to write upon its first page a few words in his beloved Arabic. In the last of all the books the words are these: "Help us, O Lord, to write thy truth enfolded by thy beauty in this book." And in an earlier one, "O my brother, every problem that has troubled you has troubled me also."

So *The Prophet* was completed and published, with the drawing of the face of Almustafa as its frontispiece, and eleven other drawings that brought to the eyes and spirit of our time a fair example of Gibran's real power. It had but been glimpsed before, not fully shown forth in its vast strength and pure beauty.

The book was received by the press critics without fan-fare or even enthusiasm, but rather with faint praise, for the most part.

This from *The Bookman:*

Oriental philosophy holds a strange fascination for occidental minds. And doubly attractive is this philosophy when it is couched in the beautifully simple poetic prose of Kahlil Gibran's "The Prophet." . . . A . . . mystical touch is imparted to the book by the twelve drawings . . . of graceful nudes rising from chaos, as if to illustrate the striving toward clarity of more or less complicated ideas.

From the London *Times:*

Kahlil Gibran is a poet of the Near East, who in this book combines all that is best in Christian and Buddhist thought in a series of replies made by a prophet Almustafa to those who question him concerning the conduct of life and the mystery of death which he feels approaching.

It would be amusing, if it were not a little pathetic, to contemplate the way the gentlemen critics, after a hearty Thursday dinner, ruffle the pages of a new book, stopping here and there to catch the drift, if possible, and then toss off a few brisk sentences for their "review," and that is that.

However, from another English paper, unidentified on the clipping, there is this word, in a review signed Y.O., to convince us that one among the critics took time out to peruse the book. He says:

I have not seen for years a book more beautiful in its thought, and when reading it I understand better than ever before what Socrates meant in the *Banquet* when he spoke of beauty of thought, which exercises a deeper enchantment than the beauty of form. . . . How profound is that irony of Gibran's about the lovers of freedom "who wear their freedom as a yoke and a handcuff."

Again, from the *Chicago Evening Post Literary Review:*

There will be very little shouting over this book, but a man's worth is not to be judged by how loudly he is shouted over. . . . Truth is here: truth expressed with all the music and beauty and idealism of a Syrian. . . . The words of Gibran bring to one's ears the majestic rhythm of Ecclesiastes. . . . For Kahlil Gibran has not feared to be an idealist in an age of cynics. Nor to be concerned with simple truth where others devote themselves to mountebank cleverness. . . . The twenty-eight chapters in the book form a little Bible, to be read and loved by those at all ready for the truth.

This man was right. There was no shouting, but there was the beginning of a whisper that persisted and grew in volume. *The Prophet* — have you heard of *The Prophet?* Have you read *The Prophet?*

It was like a little breeze that grew into a strong wind.

The book was read to hundreds of people at St. Marks

In-the-Bouwerie, as I have said, very soon after its appearance, and from that moment its message began to make its undeterred way into the consciousness of multitudes of people. It is still making its way throughout the world. The poets of other lands, the men and the women who have seen the import of the message, have taken it to their hearts and made it into their own language for their own countrymen, into more than thirty languages and dialects. And still there is no shouting, but a steady, mighty river of refreshing and enrichment for those "ready for the truth."

In 1933 it was my pleasure to address the great audience gathered to attend the World Fellowship of Faiths in Chicago. Many men and women from every cult and creed and faith on the planet were met together to speak each of his spiritual conviction. I had chosen to speak upon the topic *The Evangelism of Culture*. During the course of the half hour address I quoted from *The Prophet*, as I have never once failed to do throughout these past twenty years whenever and wherever I have had the opportunity to speak to a group or an audience.

At the close of the afternoon session of the conference, a dark-eyed young Hindu youth came to me and said, "What was the book — the name of the book — that you quoted from?" His question and my answer marked the beginning of a most precious friendship that extended over the years. The lad, Rama Murti, was the private secretary to Rajah Singh of Nepal, attending the conference with him. When they returned to India, Rama took

62

his *Prophet* and one for his younger brother, a young Hindu poet who also writes fine English poetry.

For several years the most astounding letters came from this young man. The last one told me that he was teaching English in a preparatory school in Tokyo — to the Japanese. That was four years ago. Today, I know nothing further of this beautiful young friend.

But I know that *The Prophet* had opened to him untold truth and beauty, and that his whole life, and his death, would be richer and grander than they could otherwise have been.

I have written elsewhere in this book of my own first contact with the words of Gibran, and as I write there passes through my mind, one after another, a succession of tales that have been told me of other first contacts.

I remember one January 6th, Gibran's birthday, in my studio in the old Grand Hotel in New York City. It was a high room, and long and wide, with five windows that looked out on Broadway and on 31st Street, a corner room. The unusually long windows were hung with curtains of a very fine silk pongee, and in the evening, when the street lights were on and my lights extinguished, the reflection of colours upon the walls and ceiling gave the breath-taking effect of a glowing sunset.

On this January 6th my friends were gathered with me to remember Gibran and to talk of him, and there were no lights in my room. There were twenty or more persons, and the atmosphere of the place was electric,

63

the vibration indescribably heightened. And they told, each one, how *The Prophet* had first come into their lives.

There was a young Russian girl named Marya, who had been climbing in the Rockies with a group of friends, other young people. She had gone aside from them a little and sat down on a rock to rest, and beside her she saw a black book. She opened it. There was no name, no mark in the book. It was *The Prophet*, which meant nothing to her. Idly she turned the pages, then she began to read a little, then a little more.

"Then," said Marya, telling us the story, "I rushed to my friends and shouted — I shouted, 'Come and see — what I have all my life been waiting for — I have found it — Truth!'"

Another young woman, a teacher in a private school, who is also a fine poet, had a curious story.

The room in which she was teaching was on a hallway a short distance from the outer door. One morning as she stood before her class the door of the room opened and a man, a stranger, entered holding an open book in his hand.

Without preliminary he said, "I have something to read to you, something of most vital importance," and he read aloud, forthwith, the chapter on children from *The Prophet*.

The young woman was so amazed at the proceeding, the swiftness and ardour of the visitor, as well as the words that she heard coming from his lips, that she was

64

The Great Effort

unable to utter a word. He closed the book and left the room. Thus had she come to know of the little black book.

I know a gentleman in New York City, the manager of a well-known real estate firm. He told me this: "My wife has three copies of *The Prophet* in our house. When we meet a new acquaintance who promises to be congenial, she lends him, or her, one of the copies. According to the person's reaction to the book we form our opinion of his worthwhileness."

All of these things are true, believe me, not because the book is poetry, not because of its charm and beauty, its rhythm and its music, not at all. It is because therein is written in a simple form that an intelligent child can grasp and hold in its mind and heart those things which are the most profound truth of our human existence, and the most vital. It is a living book, and it touches and stirs the spirit with a finger of fire.

You cannot read a page without being moved in the depths of your consciousness, if you are one of those "at all ready for the truth." Witness these lines:

Love one another, but make not a bond of love:
Let it rather be a moving sea between the shores of your
      souls.

Your children are not your children. . . .
They come through you but not from you,
And though they are with you yet they belong not to you.

65

You cannot separate the just from the unjust and the good from the wicked;
For they stand together before the face of the sun even as the black thread and the white are woven together.
And when the black thread breaks, the weaver shall look into the whole cloth, and he shall examine the loom also.

Your daily life is your temple and your religion.

For in that day you shall know the hidden purposes in all things,
And you shall bless darkness as you would bless light.

Work is love made visible.

VII

"A MIST CARVED INTO AN IMAGE"

The first widespread acquaintance of an American audience with the art of Gibran had come in 1919 with the publication of *Twenty Drawings*, following *The Madman* and preceding *The Forerunner*. This book, however, was really only a glimpse into the world of creation that Gibran was essaying.

There had been previous exhibitions of drawings, first in Boston and later in New York City. In the former city the always conservative *Transcript* gave the young artist significant recognition. It said:

Mr. Gibran is a young Syrian, who, in his drawings, manifests the poetical and imaginative temperament of his race, and a remarkable vein of individual invention. The . . . beauty and nobility . . . of his pictorial fancies are wonderful; and the tragic import of other conceptions is dreadful. All told, his drawings make a profound impression, and, considering his age, the qualities shown in them are extraordinary for originality and depth of symbolic significance. . . . The earnest desire to give expression to metaphysical ideas has triumphantly prevailed over technical limitations, to the extent that the imagination is greatly stirred by the abstract or moral beauty of the thought.

Even this much of comprehension was gratifying in a period when the art of the moment was far from being instinct with "moral beauty" or "symbolic significance." The drawings did make a profound impression, but a tragedy for the young artist followed hard upon the success of the exhibition. The building in which it was housed was burned to the ground, and with it the entire collection of his precious work.

It was a body blow to Gibran. It is impossible to imagine what the destruction of his early work meant to one of so sensitive and volatile a nature. But much later, after the two years spent in Paris, where he studied at the Académie Julien and painted at the Beaux Arts, he said, "The fire that burned my early paintings was a gift from the good God. *They said* it was good work, but I know now that it was green work." He said, "While I was in Paris it seemed that the mist that hung between me and Me had gone to nothingness."

In his later years he liked to talk about the years in Paris and the early years in New York, of his first studio, which he called "my little cage," and then the spacious one, higher up in the building, a great room where he felt a new freedom, where he said, "I can spread my wings."

It was in this studio that the drawing was made of the revered Abdul Baha in 1912. The saintly man had indicated that seven in the morning was the hour at which he would consent to sit for his portrait. Telling about it, Gibran said, "I remained awake all night, for I knew I should never have an eye or a hand to work with if I took my sleep."

Here also were made the drawings of the poet Yeats, of Masefield, just returned from Gallipoli "with ghosts in his eyes," of AE [George William Russell], of Laurence Housman, of Johan Bojer, of Edwin Markham, dean of American poets, of Paul Bartlett, of Percy Mackaye, of Witter Bynner, and of countless other distinguished persons.

The complete list would be a long one, astonishingly long when we consider that all the time the artist was the poet as well, writing in his beloved native Arabic and in his adopted English, of which he had acquired perfect mastery.

The first New York exhibition was held in the Montross Galleries in December of 1914. And I feel that it is significant to quote at length from a news-press article that speaks clearly and with discernment of the impression made at the time. The article appears without a byline, and with no indication of which of the metropolitan papers it was clipped from. But its content is vital. It said:

His drawings include many portrait heads of notable persons. . . . Their technical qualities, obtained solely by line work of the pencil, are extraordinarily fine; one of the methods involved being the super-imposing of the dark lines upon a ground work of half-tone lines. The result is a luminousness and vibration of color that impart a palpitating sense of livingness to the flesh, while the method also combines the rich effect of charcoal with the fugitive delicacy of silver-print.

Again, there are many drawings of Ruth St. Denis in the act of dancing; rapidly done, somewhat in Rodin's manner and with the same intention of seizing the essence of some movement in its living fluency. Further, there are studies of the nude in which the motive is the expressiveness of flesh and form and gesture. These lead on to the oil paintings, of which there are some two dozen, sufficient in number to transport us thoroughly into the world of the artist's imagination.

For it is a world of original creation that unfolds itself; a world visibly composed of mountains, scanty vegetation and sky; with feeling of solitariness, sometimes of desolation, and always, even in contracted space, with suggestion of a margin of immensity. But it needs only a little familiarity with the things seen to realize that there is symboled here a world of the spirit.

The impression of this world is elemental; as of vast forces, still inchoate, stirring in the womb of infinity in preparation for the struggle of birth. It is the symbol of the world of the spirit, as it may seem to an individual human soul awakening to the loneliness of self-consciousness in the presence of the mystery of the rhythmic oneness of life and death.

It is a world, in part, of no illusions and delusions, no sophistries, evasions, subterfuges; a naked world, tenanted with nakedness; a world of elemental instincts, as in the beginning when "they were both naked, the man and the woman and were not ashamed."

For the force, which now slumbers in, now stirs, the inhabitants of this world is the sex instinct in its most natural, that is to say, its purest appeal. It scarcely involves sex consciousness, but rather the subconscious affinity of flesh; the call of flesh to flesh, the woman's, the man's, the child's. . . .

Yet it is a world into which conflict enters. Flesh finds itself the victim of strange desires, caught in the grip of passions of bewildering violence. Moreover, there creeps into it the final bewilderment of death. The flesh of the mother lies cold and pallid on the earth into which it is about to dissolve and the rosy flesh of the child cries in vain for warmth and sustenance, a tiny foundling amid the inanimate loneliness.

It is in this last picture, called "Birth of Tragedy," that the artist has reached his profoundest note, in an exhibition distinguished throughout by profoundness of purpose and feeling. And it is an exhibition that, despite the titles attached to the pictures, avoids the banality of allegorical representation. It appeals pri-

71

marily to the aesthetic imagination through beauties of composition, color and tactile qualities, and thence by the pathways of instinct and intuition invades one's spiritual consciousness.

It is remarkable, as showing how an artist, influenced by the modern tendency to revert to the primitive and elemental, can direct it, if he have high capacity of imagination, into channels of deep significance."

There has never been, to my knowledge, any other such pellucid and penetrating utterance concerning the complete body of Gibran's work as an artist. The writer knows the scope and the achievement of the artist's dream, and has stepped over for the time being, completely into Gibran's very world. I am sure that this generous and just evaluation warmed the heart of the sensitive young painter, showing his work for the first time in the great metropolis of the Western world. And I could wish to know the name of the man who wrote it.

Three years later there was a second exhibition, this time at the Knoedler Galleries, not now by a newcomer, but by one whose place has been definitely established through a comparatively small public in and around New York City. Keen interest greeted this second showing of additional work, and this widening of interest resulted in the publication of *Twenty Drawings*, aforementioned.

This book, with its introductory essay by Alice Raphael is, so far, the only volume of reproductions without text that has come into being.

We read in the introduction:

> The qualities of the East and the West are blended in him with a singular felicity of expression, so that while he is the symbolist in the true sense of the word, he is not affixed to traditional expression, as he would be if he were creating in the manner of the East; and though he narrates a story as definitely as any pre-Raphaelite, it is without any fan-fare of historical circumstances or any of the accompaniment of symbolic accessories. In his art there is no conflict whether the idea shall prevail over the emotion, or whether the emotion shall sway the thought, because both are so equally established that we are not conscious of the one or the other as dominant. . . . In this fusion of two opposing tendencies the art of Gibran transcends the conflicts of the schools and is beyond the fixed conceptions of the classic or romantic traditions.

Twenty Drawings, opening now to the world of art the truth of the power and authority and sensitive beauty of this man's graphic skill, and also opening to simple folk to whom art is simply a word for something they do not comprehend a vista of colour and form and magic that gives them pleasure without having to understand.

Frequently some incident would occur to emphasize this attraction the pictures had for simple folk. I remember an afternoon while the exhibit was being held in Gibran's studio, the year after his death, when the little foreign woman who helped with the rough cleaning about the place, came up the stairs dressed in her Sunday best, and into the studio "to look at the exhibition — yes?" she said.

Her English was halting and queer, but her heart was warm and eager. I welcomed her as one of our guests, and she walked slowly all around the room, stopping to look, and stopping again and again. When she had been all around she came to me and said, "I go — once more — around?" "Certainly," I replied, "as often as you like." "Yes," she nodded, "then I go two times more around — isn't it?" And she did.

After the third time, and it had taken her all of three quarters of an hour, she came and took my hand. "It is to thank you," she said. "It is to tell you — I do not know it — what they say — all, but I think — they are not *just pictures*."

Not just pictures. No. As for classic, romantic, tradition, ancient, modern — she did not know the words. But she knew, and the light in her eyes revealed it, that here was something beyond and above her, yet something that held her, that spoke to her, that moved her deeply. They were not merely pencil on paper or brush on canvas, not "just pictures."

And I am sure that her reaction would have delighted Gibran more than all the erudite discussion of symbolism and mysticism and trends and verities and what-nots.

74

Gibran has said, "A work of art is a mist carved into an image." As simple as that. And again, "Art is a step from nature toward the infinite." And he took the step firmly and beautifully, grateful to those who accepted his gathered fruits, whether they might be the wise or the foolish, the scholar or the shepherd, but always with an inclination toward the foolish and the shepherd.

VIII

"IS IT THE VOICE . . . OF THE ARABIC PEOPLE?"

Early in 1919, the year in which the *Twenty Drawings* was printed, there appeared in the book section of The New York *Evening Post* a longish article by Joseph Gollomb. This article quotes Gibran extensively, and is evidently the result of a highly successful interview. It reports Gibran at his conversational best. The reviewer had quite evidently found the poet in an expansive mood, and gives us a delightful resumé.

He first contrasts Gibran and Tagore, saying:

Both have written in English with as fine a command of the Western tongue as of their own. And each is an artist in other forms besides poetry. But there the resemblances end and differences appear, the most striking being in their physical appearance. Tagore with his long, picturesque hair and beard and his flowing robe, is a figure from some canvas Sir Frederic Leighton might have painted of a religious mystic. Gibran is Broadway or Copley Square or The Strand, or the Avenue de l'Opéra — a correctly dressed cosmopolitan of the Western world.

His dark brows and moustache and somewhat curly hair above a good forehead; the clear brown eyes, thoughtful but never abstracted in expression; the sensibly tailored clothes, smart but not conspicuous — there seemed to me a chameleon-like ease of adaptiveness about him. In his studio in West Tenth Street he looked a sensible denizen of Greenwich Village. . . . But had I seen him at a congress of economists, or in a Viennese café, or in his native Syria, I feel sure he would look equally in the picture in each instance. It is not a case of lack of individuality with him but, on the contrary, an unusual common sense and sympathy which transcend differences and enable him to understand so well each environment in which he finds himself that he neither feels nor looks the stranger.

After discussing Gibran's work at length, Mr. Gollomb comes to the reporting of his words:

Notwithstanding his citizenship in the world as a whole, Mr. Gibran feels himself a Syrian. To him there is no contradiction here. He is working to bring about a world in which there is one great fellowship of understanding and sympathy.

"But in that great process the task of each people will be not to do away with its national character, but to contribute it," he said to me. "And the Arabic people have contributed much to the rest of the world and will give more. Their literature, when it comes to be known by the West, will, perhaps, be found one of the richest on earth, with the Koran as its masterpiece. Even in pre-Islamic times, the Period of Ignorance as it is called, there was a great body of poetry, very masculine, moving, and imbued with gigantic vision, that was not without its influence on the Western world. The Book of Job, for instance, is an Arabic work translated and adapted by the Hebrews.

"There was such a wealth of poetry produced that many and complex forms had to be developed as its vehicle. Remember that among Arabic peoples poetry then, as to-day, has not been confined to the cultured few but is the prized possession of the great mass of even the illiterate.

"It originated in the songs, improvisations, recitations, and stories of the pre-Mohammedan Arabs when of written literature, as far as we know, there was little or none. And much in the same way to-day our national literature spreads among the masses. For verbal memory is strong with us. Epigrams, sallies, gems of feeling which were born in improvisation, were treasured by hearers and carried home to be passed on through the generations. But the experience of all peoples is that memory has to be helped by form. So sentences became balanced. They were given definite endings. They grew short and usually carried a rhyme or an assonance. The simplest form of this in Arabic literature is the *saj*, or rhymed prose, which Mohammed used in many parts of the Koran. Then metre was introduced into the body of the sentence. From this developed other forms until even the Western world adopted some of them. For example, the sonnet was copied by the Italians from the Arabs by way of Spain.

"In the century after Mohammed, the Arabs comprised the greatest empire in the history of the world, from within sixty miles of Paris to the heart of China. And with it grew the literature and learning of the people. At that time they had the only universities in the world. They knew that the earth was round long before Galileo. And in the towers of their churches were telescopes. Later, when the Spanish came and conquered, they replaced them with church bells.

"When all Europe was dark in the eighth, ninth, and tenth centuries, the Arabs had a school of translators of Greek philosophers. Most of them were Syrians and they formed a link between Greek culture and a renaissance of Arabic culture. In the fifteenth century the Turks destroyed the Arabic empire, and its culture went into eclipse until the last eighty or one hundred years. But even in the long interim there was kept alive the fundamental virile spirit of the race through their struggle with the desert, a quality which, when poetry emerged again, gave it a stirring power.

"Of the graphic arts among Mohammedans there has been but little development because it is forbidden 'to make an image of God's work.' So that painting and sculpture are practically non-existent. But nature's forms, greatly conventionalized, have gone into

79

rug weaving and kindred art, and considerable progress has been made there. In music also the Arabs have made themselves felt by the Western world. The songs of southern Russia, for example, would be well understood and enjoyed by my people, their origin often being Arabic. Tchaikovsky and Verdi have felt its influence. 'Aïda' is composed of Arabic motifs Italianized. Debussy told me that he, too, had taken our motifs and built upon them some of his works.

"The renaissance in Arabic culture which has taken place within the last century has a strong admixture of Western influences. Certainly we are acquainted with your best. In Syria and Egypt we know, Dante, Shakespeare, Hugo, the French poets from Villon to Maeterlinck. And it would not surprise me if a survey of how widely Shakespeare is known among us were to show that we read him as much as you do, if not more. The average educated man in Syria knows at least English and French in addition to his own language. And there are few in Mount Lebanon — I speak from personal experience — who not only do not read great foreign literature but also memorize it and sing it; for remember, literature is largely vocal with us.

"Until the coming of the Allied armies in the great war the Arabs were under the yoke of one of the most ruthless despots in history. Now that the yoke of Turkey is off our people our hope of self-determination is strong. We will seek guidance, of course, and one of

80

the Allied nations, perhaps France, will take us by the hand. If so, and the natural reciprocal exchange of national cultures takes place, our people will have much to give.

"There is an enormous body of romantic and epic poetry locked up in our language. There is a more brilliant Arabian Nights left untranslated in our literature than even that which you know. There is a precious store of mystical philosophy hitherto untapped by outsiders. And when all this wealth is added to the culture of the world, it will be found to be the contribution of a great people."

In conclusion Mr. Gollomb poses his penetrating question:

Mr. Gibran was born within a mile of the famous Cedars of Lebanon. He is emerging into citizenship of the whole new world. Is it Kahlil Gibran, the individual, who is thus emerging? Or is it the voice and genius of the Arabic people?

Whatever the answer to this query may be, this much is true, there is no other name which has come into world eminence from the Arabic people to occupy such a high place, and to command such a vast audience, not in the full century of the renaissance of that remarkable people. I am personally grateful to Mr. Gollomb for his preservation, in the files of his paper, of this extremely informative and delightful report of his session with Gibran.

IX

"WORDS ARE TIMELESS"

On a Sunday afternoon in the Autumn of 1925 I went for an hour or two to the studio at the invitation of Gibran, who, by-the-way, never during the course of our friendship took the acceptance of such an invitation for granted. He would say, over the telephone, "If you are free would you like to spend a little time with a weary man?" And how soul-weary I often found him!

On that day the door was ajar, as always. Knocking and entering, I saw him sitting at his table writing. I said nothing, took my accustomed seat and waited.

Presently he greeted me, and then said, "I am making a poem. It is about a blind poet."

Then he rose and walked up and down the room for several minutes before he again seated himself at the table and wrote a line or two.

I waited while he repeated his writing and his walking again and again. Then a thought came to me. The next time he walked I went and seated myself at his table and took up his pencil. When he turned he saw me sitting there.

"You make the poem and I'll write it," I said.

"No — no. You shall not write for me. You must write your own poems."

"But I would so love to write your words. And see how simple — you walk up and down and talk it — and I'll put it down! It's a game."

"I could never work with anyone — like that," he said.

"Make believe I'm not anyone — just a little mechanical machine — "

"You — you are a very stubborn woman," he said, almost angrily.

"I can't help it," I answered. "I was a very stubborn little girl!"

He drew in his breath as if he were going to give me a real blast of his anger. Then suddenly he laughed — we both laughed, and the matter was settled. He walked and talked the poem, and I wrote. And from that time on the work was done that way.

He completed the poem, *The Blind Poet,* very slowly, with long pauses between the lines, composing in Arabic as was his inevitable custom, and translating carefully into English.

At the end he came and looked down on the page and said, "I have always declared I could never work with another — to make my poems. That is why I will never have a secretary here when I am working. Perchance, I have been mistaken. . . . Well, you and I are two poets working together." He paused. Then after a si-

83

lence, "We are friends," he said. "I want nothing from you, and you want nothing from me. We share life."

And I remembered the line in *The Prophet* that says, "And let there be no purpose in friendship save the deepening of the spirit."

That was Gibran's kind of friendship.

And here is the poem made and written down that day.

The Blind Poet

I have been blinded by light,
The very sun that gave you your day
Gave me my night, deeper than dream.

And yet I am a wayfarer,
While you would sit where life gave you birth
Until death comes to give you another birth.

And yet I would seek the road
With my lyre and my staff,
While you sit and tell your beads.
And yet I would go forth in darkness
Even when you fear the light.

And I would sing.

I cannot lose my way.
Even when there is no sun
God sees our path and we are safe.
And though my feet shall stumble
My song shall be wingéd upon the wind.

I have been blinded by gazing
At the deep and the high.
And who would not yield his eyes
For a sight of the high and the deep?
Who would not blow out two little
    flickering candles
For a glimpse of the dawn?

You say, "Pity he cannot see the stars,
Nor the buttercups in the fields."

And I say, "Pity they cannot reach the stars,
And hear the buttercups.
Pity they have no ears within their ears.
Pity, pity they have no lips
Upon their finger-tips."

The poem was printed soon thereafter in an issue of
The New Orient, a cultural magazine published at that
time by Syud Hossain, a distinguished Muslim writer
and editor, and a lecturer of international eminence.
With the poem was the reproduction of a drawing that
Gibran called *The Blind Poet and His Mother*.

It now seemed very natural and simple for me to continue taking down words that came from the poet's lips,
often in ordinary conversation, though ordinary conversation with Kahlil Gibran was anything but ordinary. I
kept a notebook within reach of my hand, and would jot
down a sentence or two, not unnoticed, however; for he

would say, "Are you remembering everything I say, against me?"

It was then that I determined, if I could be accorded the wisdom and the sense, that I would sometime write about this man, of whom nothing had been, or to this day has been, written in English save a few interviews, scattered opinions in the public press, and a brief essay or two by a priest or a rabbi.

I told him of my determination and he was pleased. He accepted my purpose like a child who has heard a piece of happy news. And it was from that time on that he talked often of his childhood, of his mother, and also of things that he would wish to have remembered "if they remember me at all." He would frequently preface such a tale with the words, "If I should die tonight remember this — " And these are the things, many of them, that are written in this book.

It was at that time, also, that the idea occurred to me to gather up the choice words that were spoken during the hours in the studio, together with the hosts of sayings I had found jotted down on a slip or scrap of paper here and there in all sorts of places, and to make them into a volume. Gibran ridiculed the idea at first, and he said, "They would only be so much sand and foam." Here was the title for the book — so *Sand and Foam* it became, and he began to take an interest in it. He would give me, a little shyly, a piece of a theatre program, a bit of cardboard from the end of a cigarette-box, a torn envelope, with lines written on them, and say, "Here you are —

foolishly gathering sand and foam!" But he thoroughly enjoyed it, and began making sentences — some of them comparable with the most powerful things he has ever said or written, and they are contained in the volume.

One day he said, "Please write this — and remember — it must be the last word in the book: Every thought I have imprisoned in expression I must free by my deeds."

And for the first saying, he wrote:

> I am forever walking upon these shores,
> Betwixt the sand and the foam.
> The high tide will erase my foot-prints,
> And the wind will blow away the foam.
> But the sea and the shore will remain
> Forever.

At length I had collected a creditable number of these sayings, and I typed them and took them to the studio. Gibran took the manuscript and seated himself. For a half hour he turned the pages. Neither one of us spoke a word. Then he looked up, and with a look of wonder upon his face, he said, "Have I indeed made all this, or have you helped me along?"

"Not a word is mine," I answered, "and you know it. Every line in those pages is Gibran, they could be no one else."

Sand and Foam was given to the publisher and came out in 1926, subtitled *A Book of Aphorisms*.

"Do we have to say *Aphorisms*?" the poet asked.

"Why may we not use the nice, simpler word *sayings?*" But the verdict being against the simpler word, it was thrown out. However Gibran always called it "The Little Book of Sayings."

It is my opinion, and I have often heard others express it as their own, that there is not in the language another book of its character, a book that has not only three dimensions — height, depth, and breadth — but also the fourth dimension, timelessness, which is but another word for time unbounded, limitless.

Therein are brief sentences that give expression to the wisdom of the ages — and I use the phrase in its basic sense, not as the catchword from any cult — and in the form of pure truth to which no faith or creed will wish to take exception:

If your heart is a volcano how shall you expect flowers to bloom in your hands?

He who can put his finger upon that which divides good from evil is he who can touch the very hem of the garment of God.

They say the nightingale pierces his bosom with a thorn when he sings his love song. So do we all. How else should we sing?

Though the wave of words is forever upon us, yet our depth is forever silent.

88

Faith is an oasis in the heart which will never be reached by the caravan of thinking.

Generosity is not in giving me that which I need more than you do, but it is in giving me that which you need more than I do.

It is indeed misery if I stretch an empty hand to men and receive nothing; but it is hopelessness if I stretch a full hand and find none to receive.

Mr. Hossain asked me for a review of the book for his magazine, and what was written then is as fair a presentation as I can give.
The review said:

"Words are timeless. You should utter them or write them with a knowledge of their timelessness." This line defines perhaps, if one line can define, the vast consciousness of this Lebanese poet concerning the power and purpose of human utterance.
The jacket of the book says the author "is a philosopher at his window commenting on the scene passing below." A nicely turned phrase, but the author himself said, "I would walk with all those who walk. I would not stand still to watch the procession passing by."
And the record written in these brief sentences and occasional parables, is of one who had laid his hand

upon the pulse of life, who has eaten its bread and drunk its cup, not of one who has watched and commented.

Kahlil Gibran, master of Arabic, has given the discerning English public in this fourth English book, something entirely unlike any other volume of "sayings" in the language. He has done again what he did in *The Prophet*, clothed for us what has been shown him of "the things that are between birth and death," but the garments are different.

The treatment of the ancient wisdoms concerning the realities is of the simplest, expressing the belief that "we shall never understand one another until the language is reduced to seven words." And one ponders this as one looks upon the seven drawings. Gibran's brush is his other scepter.

"Man is two men. One is awake in darkness, and the other is asleep in light." The sculptural quality in this swift stroke is seen throughout the eighty-some pages of the little book. And reading them gives one the feeling of having walked through a corridor, spacious and high, with simple truth graven in marble pictures along its walls.

Sand and Foam is a book that will penetrate the consciousness deeply and inevitably, as *The Prophet* has done.

I have quoted in the above the saying about "seven words." And I well remember an evening when the ones

90

that I have called "the seven words of Gibran" were pronounced in the studio.

We were pausing after a longish period of work, and entirely without preliminary the poet asked, "Suppose you were compelled to give up — to forget, all the words you know except seven — what are the seven words that you would keep?" With very little hesitation I chose the words, *God, life, love, beauty, Earth* — and then I could not find the two more words to make seven. So I said, "Tell me what your words would be."

"You have forgotten the most important words of all," he said, "without which the rest are impotent." That amazed me — but he went on, "The two most important words to keep are *you* and *I* — without those two there would need to be no others. *We must be* and we must *take*." Then he spoke slowly and almost breathlessly. "These are my seven words: "You, I, take, God, love, beauty, Earth."

For a long time we sat there. I cannot remember any other silence quite so long and quite so throbbing, so thrilling. I went over and over the words in my mind. It was all there — everything, all of life, and all of death which is but a part of life, and of eternity, which is God.

After a time when speech came back slowly to our lips, we took these words and made of them a small poem, taking the liberty of using the objective *me*, but adding nothing to the content of the seven words. This is the poem:

Love, take me.
Take me, Beauty.
Take me, Earth.
I take you,
Love, Earth, Beauty.
I take
God.

X

"THE CONTINUITY OF LIFE"

I know a child, a young boy of seven years, who is thrilled with the knowledge that his life is set in an orbit, "just like the stars and the planets," he says wonderingly; and that to make his life the shining thing that it is meant to be he must follow that orbit. "The Earth can't wander from its orbit," he says, "I can — but *I mustn't*."

I have asked myself a thousand times, why — how in the destiny of worlds — should my path have accorded with this other path for a time in this present?

One evening when we were doing *Sand and Foam*, I piled cushions on the floor and sat upon them instead of occupying my usual chair. Then I had a strange feeling of familiarity about the gesture, and I said, "I feel as if I've sat like this beside you many times — but I really haven't."

He waited a moment — as he so often did before replying — and I often wondered if he were thinking his reply in Arabic. Then he said, "We have done this a thousand years ago, and we shall do it a thousand years hence."

And during the writing of *Jesus, The Son of Man,* the

93

drama of some incident, now and again, was so over-whelming that I felt, and said, "It is so real. It seems as if I had been there." And his answer came, almost like a cry, "You were there! And so was I!"

Thus Gibran expressed over and over again, his utter belief in what he called "the continuity of life." The Theosophist, the Rosicrucian, certain cults, and divers other trends of thought and belief, call it reincarnation. He never used the word. It was his profound certainty that the life that is the human spirit has lived and shall live timelessly, that the bonds of love, devotion, and friendship shall bring together these endlessly reborn beings, and that animosity, evil communications, and hatred have the same effect of reassembling groups of entities from one cycle to another. Indifference acts as a separating influence. Those souls who neither love nor hate, but remain entirely self-contained as regards one another, meet but once in the pattern of the ages.

These were his beliefs — this was his faith — changeless as day and night, and as forthright. He used none of the cultist phrases and catchwords. He belonged to no sect. He had no ism.

The question has been constantly asked me, "But was not Gibran really a Christian?" My own reply would be that he was the greatest Christian of them all — but neither an organized nor an orthodox Christian. Perhaps if we must have a word — he did not need one — we might call him a Christian mystic. For mystic he certainly was in the perfect and perfected sense.

94

Crucified

When someone asked him, "What is a mystic?" he smiled and said, "Nothing very secret nor formidable — just someone who has drawn aside *one more veil*."

He once said, "Three times have I seen Him, our Lord and Brother. I have spoken with him."

And who are we to doubt? Did not Jesus Himself say to his disciples, "These things ye shall do, and greater things than these, because I go to my Father"?

Gibran also — only once in all the seven years — spoke of three mystical experiences, saying from the depth of his human burden and weariness, "This once in my life I must speak of these things to one other human being. *But you will never speak of them* — not even when I am dead."

I sat as still as a stone and listened, and I knew — for I, too, am not unacquainted with mystic vision and power — that it was eternal truth that he spoke, and that I shall never speak.

Speaking before a large audience once in a Western city, I was interrupted — politely — at a point in my talk by the same question, "Is Gibran a Christian?" I replied, as I had often before replied: "If you mean is he a communicant of the Christian Church, he is not, nor of any church; if you mean does he accept the dogmatic, directive and governing principles of any so-called Christian creed, he does not, nor of any creed. When he is pressed concerning the miracle of the immaculate conception, he replies, 'Is not every conception a miracle?' He regards Jesus as the most humanly enlightened, the most divinely informed being who has ever visited this planet, as a being of illimitable, immeasurable wisdom and might, a supreme poet, a figure of lonely power, a man whose concept of human endowments and human responsibilities was complete and convincing. Gibran believes that Jesus lived his human life to the full, that there was no cup of human rapture that he did not drink, no extremity of human anguish that he did not comprehend and share in his divinity, and that withal there was no shadow, no blemish upon his life."

This reply did not and does not satisfy orthodoxy, but it satisfied Gibran.

Having been born of parents who were Maronite Christians, he had received the religious instruction and training of their faith. He had many a tender story to tell of a priest, Father Yusef, who came sometimes to the little village of Bsherri during his travels from town to town administering the sacraments and the comfort of his counsel to his people. The child Gibran would watch for Father Yusef, and would follow him about, or walk beside him, the small hand in the big firm one, asking questions and pondering the answers.

"It was from him I learned to know God and the angels," he said. "Father Yusef was very close to God. I often looked at him curiously, and I remember once I asked him, 'Are you yourself, or are you — God?' He seemed so wonderfully good and perfect to me; I loved him with a passion that still moves me when I think of him. It was his closeness to God — through him I was feeling the love of God. . . . He did not tell me the things that I learned in the little church, but about the things in the above-world, things that I could neither see nor hear, but that I could feel in my heart. And sometimes my young heart longed to go and find those things in the above-world, rather than to stay here, where I felt a strange loneliness and an unchildish sorrow."

Even the child Gibran did not conform. He was not born into the close of the nineteenth century world to conform; he was sent as a missioner from God to re-form the human conception of the essence of life and being for those who have ears to hear, and to instruct the adventuring spirit to make its way among the starry reaches of God's infinite plan and pattern for the children of men.

Walking beside Father Yusef in his childhood Gibran found himself outside the religious faith to which he had been born. And he found no other organized and formulated "religion" that he could embrace.

From his earliest years his passionate devotion was given to Jesus, of whom he said in his youth that He was "the most supremely good and wise of all the wise and good who have walked the Earth; Jesus, our Lord and our Brother; Jesus, the Son of Man." Let us say it plainly, not sidestepping or avoiding his position, for Gibran never did. The height reached after a long continuity of lives, wherethrough all wisdom and all virtue and all power and glory possible to the human expression of God the Father had been gathered as a mighty

97

and eternal harvest — this was Gibran's Jesus, the Son of Man.

He knew that he had been upon the Earth during the period when Jesus lived in his country. He felt that Jesus had certainly visited the North Country, Lebanon, and he said, "I have seen him there. *I know.*"

These things were in the innermost of his heart and being. He did not talk of them often, but when he did he was like a man touched with the Finger of divine fire, and I could no more have doubted than I could doubt my own existence. I also remembered, and the studio high up in the old building became like a green hill in a far country which, at that time, I had not seen in this life. At moments like these, rare but intensely real and living, I did not question why I should be with this poet at this time. I knew. We had indeed lived and moved through the same scenes, a thousand, two thousand years ago.

These exalted experiences came during the writing of the book, *Jesus, The Son of Man*. To have seen him for one hour during the incalculable travail that resulted in the volume was to know that this man from Lebanon was in truth of a stuff more divinely woven, and of a pattern more godlike than our own. To have seen him thus transfigured before human eyes was to accept the certainty of his calling, the chosen and the beloved of the high gods.

XI

"OUR FRIEND AND BROTHER"

The book *Jesus* had been in Gibran's intention for a long time. He had said, "Some day, some time, we shall write of Our Friend and Brother. In five years, perhaps, or ten — "

Then without warning, on the evening of the 12th of November, 1926, came the moment that will live in my memory as long as that memory remains a living force. Gibran had been walking restlessly up and down the room, speaking haltingly of the book then foremost in his thought, *The Garden of the Prophet*. Suddenly he stopped, and a strange dark look came over his face, a curious transformation, the sort of mask that I knew from experience foretold some swift and startling utterance.

The room became filled with the heightened vibration that I had also come to know well. I opened the brown notebook at my side.

He bent his head; his face became drawn and old, the glow and beauty faded to a gray, sharp, and piteous contour, and his head shook like that of an aged and disconsolate being. Then came a voice — not Gibran's voice — but quavering, thin, and broken. Its pain and despair went through my heart like a rapier. The voice began, "It was fifty years ago tonight — the memory is like a scorpion coiled about my heart! It is like a cup more bitter than wormwood — it has blackened all my days and desecrated all my dawns — a thousand times I have been visited by the return of that night — " Then he was silent. He paced and said the words again. I wrote them down. Yet again he repeated the words.

I sat like one mesmerized as the strange tragic voice went on with a lamentation so terrible and so anguished that my own heart was wrung for this human being whom I did not know, but whose agony seemed strangely not strange to me. I could not write.

Then almost as suddenly as he had become this alien man, Gibran returned to himself, and going to his chair sat down, in silence, and closed his eyes. When he opened them, he looked at me with perfect naturalness and said, "Do you know . . . who I was?"

"No," I said.

He answered in a voice of musing, a voice with distance in it, "I was Judas. Poor Judas. . . . Suppose he had not done away with his life? Suppose he had lived on for fifty years, a hundred years, what would that life have been?"

He stood, very still and erect. His face had the look of a tormented angel. There was anguish and exaltation upon him. Then with an almost blinding illumination of his changeful face he cried out, "I can begin writing That Book tonight!"

And that night he began That Book, *Jesus, The Son of Man,* which he had been keeping in his heart for years. But the first chapter that was spoken and written was not the story of Judas, but the story from the lips of James, the son of Zebedee. Pacing up and down, speaking slowly, not in his accustomed voice or manner, weighing the English words as he spoke them, he composed the opening chapter of the book. But it was hardly composition: he was living it — he was relating the tale as though he were indeed James, who quoted the words of his Lord:

Think you that I came down the years to rule an ant-hill for a day? My throne is a throne beyond your vision. Shall he whose wings encircle the earth seek shelter in a nest abandoned and forgotten? . . . Too many are the worms that crawl about my feet, and I will give them no battle. . . . Your priest and your emperor would have my blood. They shall be satisfied ere I go hence. I would not change the course of the law. And I will not govern folly. Let ignorance reproduce itself until it is weary of its own offspring. . . . My kingdom is not of the earth. My kingdom shall be where two or three of you shall meet in love, and in wonder at the loveliness of life, and in good cheer, and in remembrance of me.

Reading the entire chapter through, it seems incredible, even to me who heard it, that such an utterance could come from the heart and lips of a man, pouring forth with such force and impact of sequence and structure. But there it is, and that is how it was done. And when Gibran did come at length to write the story of Judas, the character he gave him was not that of the man who lived through an eternity of hideous years, but rather of the one who threw himself from the High Rock, and was dashed to his death.

I have said that that night, November 12th, was a night never to be forgotten. For eighteen months the work went on. My pencil took down the words. My eyes saw that face — they still see it — which was like a battleground that would change with lightning swiftness and expression. A radiance would shine upon his countenance, from which one was constrained to turn away. His great soul was laid bare. He was transfigured, and not to be regarded of human eyes.

Each of the seventy characters came alive in that place. Each voice spoke through the lips of this man from Lebanon. Many times the exhaustion at the end of the telling was so complete as to be frightening. Sometimes, a few times, a Light, tenuous but clearly visible, showed above and about him as he walked. Only once I alluded to the Light. He had stopped pacing, and stood to speak a low, slow sentence. I looked up and saw the Light. It was almost unbearably clear and dazzling white, and I said, in spite of myself, "Kahlil! The Light!"

He started, drew in a great breath, and turned away, beginning his pacing again. And the Light faded.

And so to the completion of the volume. And when it was finished, the last fair copy typed and ready for the

102

publisher, it was as though both the poet and the one whose hand had transcribed the record had come through a mighty and terrible struggle, and were wounded to the very heart. But somehow the memory was, and is, magnificent; and the wounds, and the scars they left are a part of the great treasure of a rich and incomparable experience.

It is to be remembered also that the drawings that are reproduced in the book were made during the same period of time.

I wish to speak in particular of the drawing of the head of Jesus, which had been placed as the frontispiece of the volume.

I saw the very beginning of this conception of the Son of Man. One evening Gibran took a heavy art board large enough for a life-sized head, and placed it upon his easel. His manner was breathless, as if he were handling something alive.

I suppose I looked at him with a question in my eyes. One seldom questioned Gibran when he was working. One never dreamed of saying, "What are you going to do?"

He held up before my eyes a stub of a pencil, not two inches long, and pointed to the board. Then, placing two fingers upon his lips, enjoining silence, he began at the top of the board, and with incredible swiftness, in the briefest moment, there was drawn the clear, definite, beautiful line of the profile of that Face. The drawing was begun.

The board stood upon the easel for many days and many nights. From time to time the artist would go and stand before it, touching it with his pencil, brushing it with his small bit of black artist's gum, or modeling with the flat of his thumb. Then he would walk again, telling more of the story that was in the process of coming to life.

Sometimes this walking and working and stopping and walking again would go on for hours, into the deep of the night, even frequently until the worker, glancing up at his skylight, would say in surprise, "Look! The window is white!" It was indeed, for dawn was beginning to come, and the work had gone on all night.

He would sometimes say, "And are you still here? And have I been telling you tales all this time? Forgive me — you must be weary almost unto death."

I was, but I always contrived to give him a quick denial, "No — not tired at all. But you — "

"I — I am already dead," he would say, the spell broken, and a weary but radiant smile replacing the strained, gray look he had been wearing. Then he would drop, fully clothed, onto the wide divan, dropping off his slippers as he did so, asleep almost before his head rested upon the pillow. A huge soft blanket drawn up to protect him as he slept, and he never heard the soft closing of the door as I staggered out into the dawn and through the throbbing silence of those streets, downtown New York, where no human being seemed to be stirring — around the corner to the comfort of my own little place in the old and gracious Hotel Brevoort. But that moment with the dawn, the sky above Manhattan, the misty Washington Arch at the Square, and having them all to myself — it was like a benediction to a service of worship, and I never cared how many or how long the hours of work might be.

And then, at last, the Head, as well as the script, was finished. There was an incident connected with the bringing out of the book that was disturbing at the time, but has eventually resulted in making the Face of Gibran's Jesus familiar to hundreds, yes thousands, of young men and women from all parts of the world.

The drawing, when taken to the publisher's, disappointed those who had the directing of the illustrative material. The line of the head at the top and at the back was "incomplete." That is, the head was not quite all visible on the board.

The drawing was brought back to the studio — and Gibran said, in a strange, veiled voice, "They say we did not give our Jesus a big enough board." He was touched in the very center of his artist's sense of beauty and proportion. However, there was no way of changing the drawing even if he had wished to do so. So he drew a second head, the one that appears in the volume, giving "our Jesus a larger board!" There was irony in his voice, and there was a tenseness in his drawing hand as he worked to complete the material to the satisfaction of the art critics.

The first, the original, Gibran always called "our Jesus." The second is entirely lacking in the touch of fire and furious creation through which the original was born. It is not alive. It is a copy, with no grace of inspiration.

I had been bitterly angry, and wanted to fight the critical opinion. But Gibran would not have it so. He smiled with his lips, though his eyes burned with weary fire, and he said, "Will you accept Him? Do you mind that the board was too small?"

So the greatest treasure of the collection came into my grateful possession. Much later it went with me across the water and was shown to silent hundreds in England — in London and in a half dozen English villages, among them my family home village of Bideford in lovely Devon. Everywhere it was the same: "This is how He must have looked." And in Paris, when it became known that this now famous drawing was in that city, my little apartment on the rue Michel Ange was besieged by visitors.

Back in the United States, during journeys to many American cities, the drawing always had the same impact on those who came to see. In Cleveland the pastor of one of the great churches brought his two little children to see the Face. The boy, eight years old, looked for a time in silence, then he said, softly, "Oh! . . . Oh, Daddy, *that is the way He looked!* Why didn't the other people ever make the picture right, before?"

And a lad of about sixteen, in the same city, a gay

106

Jesus, the Son of Man

youngster, full of *joie de vivre* said, "Well . . . I'm not religious — and I don't want to be. But I could go for a Jesus like that one."

And finally the drawing of Jesus, The Son of Man, was presented as a gift to International House on Riverside Drive, in New York City, through which thousands of eager and ardent young people of many nations pass each year. And there it may be seen, and is seen daily through eyes from the far corners of the Earth, and apprehended by hearts that will never forget what they have seen in that Face.

Rereading the book entire, as I have done during the past few days, I am again visited by that first amazement which overcame me as I listened to it through those days and nights of its composition. I hear the words spoken aloud, and I hear also the voice of the poet saying, as he frequently did say, after some utterance of shattering power, "My God! I did not know I was going to say that."

I know now that the book will never be a book to me, but always a host of living entities, breathing and vocal. And not because of Kahlil Gibran, my well-beloved friend, but rather because of the livingness of Anna, the mother of Mary; of Matthew and the Sermon on the Mount; of Joseph of Arimathaea, reporting the words of Jesus; of Susannah of Nazareth, and her story of the Mother of Jesus; of Mary Magdalen, and of Cyborea, the mother of Judas.

It is these who live upon the pages of this book, not

107

the great man who loved them into being. Gibran has done his work supremely well. It has been done with single power by one fully conscious of the social and political and religious Palestine and Syria and Rome of that period, one who was at home in the richness and significance of the traditions and in the history and the language of the country of Jesus. The Aramaic that Jesus spoke was Gibran's other language. The atmosphere and the aspect of the Land of Judea is cast like a spell upon the reader who, moving through the scenes of those days and that country, is aware of far more than the words upon the printed page. We behold the Young Man of Nazareth as we have never beheld Him, for in this *Jesus* of Gibran's, for the first time since the writings of the Gospels, a countryman of Jesus writes of his words and deeds.

Many men all down the ages have essayed to write of that great drama enacted two thousand years ago. The past ten decades have given to the world more literature concerning Him than any ten decades since His death. Men are still writing the story.

But not as this man. His story has been given to the tongues of those who knew Him or knew of Him. Seventy human beings, both His friends and His enemies, Roman, Greek, Jew, Persian, Babylonian, priest and poet and Pharisee — each tells his own tale, and the voices ring in our ears. Gibran has made what we may call a redistribution of certain sayings and doings related in the four Gospels, and has restated them in his own way.

I have heard the book spoken of frequently, as "the Gospel according to Gibran."

In the *Manchester Guardian*, a reviewer wrote of the book thus:

It is a great delight to the jaded reader, wandering about in the endless forest of books which has sprung up around the Four Gospels, to come suddenly upon one that has great beauty and distinction peculiarly its own. Such a book I have just found in *Jesus, The Son of Man: His words and deeds as recorded by those who knew Him*, by Kahlil Gibran. It is not another *Life of Jesus* after the fashion of those which Renan and Farrar and Sanday and Headham and many others have made familiar. Rather it is of the nature of an imaginative reconstruction, in which the mind of a great poet has used, without limiting himself to, the materials to be found in the Gospels. . . .

Kahlil Gibran has seen Jesus, and helps others to see Him. Even the hostile voices have their contribution in the interpretation, for they reveal the forces that drove Jesus to His doom. "He was a magician, warp and woof," snarls a young Priest in Capernaum. "He juggled with the words of our prophets, and the sanctities of our forefathers. . . ."

But naturally it is his friends who are his truest interpreters. "Once," says Rumanous, a Greek poet, "I too deemed myself a poet. But when I stood before Him in Bethany I knew what it is to hold an instrument with but a single string before one who commands all instruments."

This is a book for those who can read with understanding.

John Haynes Holmes writing his review of the book said in part:

Kahlil Gibran has attempted a unique and daring experiment. . . . If any man were fitted to attempt this adventurous task it is Mr. Gibran. . . . It is as though a contemporary [of Jesus] sat down at a belated hour, to write another and different Gospel. . . . Now and again the poet dares a direct comparison with the New Testament, as in the parable of the shepherd in South Lebanon. I heard Gibran read this parable once, and I thought then, as I think now, that it matches the Scripture standard.

Gibran, in the making of this book, felt that he was a contemporary of those others who speak their memories of the young Galilean. And finally, *A Man from Lebanon, Nineteen Centuries Afterward* speaks in words seven times refined of the Young Man, the Master Poet who was hung upon a cross outside the wall of Jerusalem, upon the Hill of the Skull:

Master, Master Singer,
Master of words unspoken,
Seven times was I born, and seven times have
    I died

Since your hasty visit and our brief welcome.
And behold I live again,
Remembering a day and a night among
    the hills,
When your tide lifted us up.
Thereafter many lands and many seas
    did I cross,
And wherever I was led by saddle
    or sail
Your name was prayer or argument.
Men would bless you or curse you;
The curse, a protest against failure,
The blessing, a hymn of the hunter
Who comes back from the hills
With provision for his mate.

And to Kahlil Gibran this "remembering a day and a night among the hills" was not merely poetry. It was remembrance, as vivid and as living as any remembrance of his childhood or youth. It was reality.

XII

"WHEN THE NIGHT OF THE TWELFTH AEON FELL"

The Earth Gods, the last book to be published while Gibran was still in this world, came into the poet's hands two weeks before he was to lay aside all earthly volumes.

He took the latest little black book, turned the pages musingly, and read aloud, softly, as if to himself, and in a strangely distant voice:

> We shall pass into the twilight;
> Perchance to wake to the dawn of another world.
> But love shall stay,
> And his finger-marks shall not be erased.
>
> The blessed forge burns,
> The sparks rise, and each spark is a sun.
> Better it is for us, and wiser,
> To seek a shadowed nook and sleep in
>   our earth divinity,
> And let love, human and frail, command
>   the coming day.

He had a peculiar feeling of tenderness for this book, unlike what he felt for any of the others. "Because," he said, "it was written out of the poet's hell — a process of child-birth and child-bearing."

In New York, in 1914–15, he had written perhaps two thirds of the book, "trying to learn to express myself directly in English." In reading the pages of this volume, it becomes evident that as a teacher of English this Lebanese was a glorious success. It is, in my opinion, one of the greatest poems in the language.

When he first brought it to light, more than a year after his *Jesus* was published, showing it rather shyly, he said, "Sometime we shall finish it — if we think it is worthy to be finished."

He had almost forgotten its existence. Like *The Prophet*, it had been put away for more than ten years. But now he read it aloud, and I was immediately consumed with a great urge for him to complete it. He resisted for some time, saying, "Will you give me no rest?" and then smiling, for rest was only a word to Gibran, and if he were not working furiously on *Earth Gods*, he would be working on some other, and he knew it as well as I.

Without the slightest delay, as if he had laid the manuscript down but yesterday, he took up his pacing and went on with the poem, beginning with the words of the Second God:

> To be, to rise, to burn before the burning sun,
> To live, and to watch the nights of the living
> As Orion watches us!

To face the four winds with a head crowned
    and high,
And to heal the ills of man with our
    tideless breath!
The tentmaker sits darkly at his loom,
And the potter turns his wheel unaware;
But we, the sleepless and the knowing,
We are released from guessing and from chance.
We pause not nor do we wait for thought.
We are beyond all restless questioning.
Be content and let the dreaming go.
Like rivers let us flow to ocean
Unwounded by the edges of the rocks;
And when we reach her heart and are merged
No more shall we wrangle and reason of
    tomorrow.

The canvas for this work is of a magnitude difficult to
portray. It begins thus:

When the night of the twelfth aeon fell,
And silence, the high tide of night,
    swallowed the hills,
The three earth-born gods, the Master
    Titans of life,
Appeared upon the mountains.

Rivers ran about their feet;
The mists floated across their breasts,

And their heads rose in majesty above
  the world.

Then they spoke, and like distant thunder
Their voices rolled over the plains.

Here are three Earth-gods, one who is weary from
aeons of ruling, one who is ambitious still to rule, and
one, young and eager, who has discovered that there is
love upon the Earth and that it is more to be desired
than the ruling of any planet. The two pay no heed to
the words of their younger brother, but only to their
own passions and their own diverse reasoning.

It is the magnitude of their concept and their argument that gives to this poem its epic quality. Here the
poet has made exposition of his own concept of the three-
fold man projected beyond himself into a state of god-
likeness. It is a daring and challenging premise. It is you
and you and I at our extreme point of comprehension,
and yet true in every point to our unspoken, even unrec-
ognized reality of entity.

The closing lines, which the poet had read aloud as
he opened the book, beginning, "We shall pass into the
twilight," and ending on the great note, the climax of
his vastest dream, "And let love, human and frail,
command the coming day," contain the epitome of Gibran's faith for the future of Earth life.

The Earth Gods is, perhaps, a book for the mystic, a

poet's book for poets, for the initiate and the dreamer of vast dreams. Yet I have known those who pride themselves on being highly practical and feet-on-the-ground, who disown any bent toward the mystical and the occult, to pronounce it a book of wonder and power. And a child of seven to whom I have read portions of the poem on request, says unvaryingly, "Read it again!" This, perhaps, for the music and the almost unearthly beauty of rhythm.

When the new copies of this book came to the author's table, there remained the completed manuscript for one more volume, a book of parables called *The Wanderer*. It was the last bit of work to be done under his own hand. It is rather a slight book in comparison with those that immediately preceded it, but no piece of writing ever came from his heart without its own peculiar beauty and glory. Of this book Claude Bragdon said, "His power came from great reservoir of Spiritual life, else it could not have been so universal and so potent, but the majesty and beauty of the language with which he clothed it were all his own."

There is a chief character here, as in *The Prophet*. This time he is a nameless man called *The Wanderer*, and of him we read:

I met him at the crossroads, a man with but a cloak and a staff, and a veil of pain upon his face. And we greeted one another, and I said to him, "Come to my house and be my guest."

116

And he came. . . .

He told us many a tale that night and also the next day, but what I now record was born out of the bitterness of his days . . . and these tales are of the dust and patience of his road.

There are fifty or more of these tales of *The Wanderer*, each one woven of the very fabric of Eastern thought and phraseology. Nothing of the West is here. It is as though, with his life drawing to its close, his native mood and atmosphere occupied the poet's being, even as it did his constant thought and conversation. For more and more he talked of his childhood and his youth, of his mother, of Father Yusef, and of another, whom he called "the only man who ever taught me anything" in college days. This man was Father Haddad of the Madrasat Al-Hikmat, the present College de la Sagesse in Beirut.

There is a return of the irony that met our eye in *The Madman*. The poet has taken a whip of slender cords, and uses it. There is a pungency in many of the tales that bespeaks weariness in the face of the stupidities and blindnesses of the world. It is a book to which one turns not for the encouragement of a quiet and tranquil spirit, but for vindication of an attitude of unrest and disillusionment.

For example, the parable of *The Full Moon:*

The full moon rose in glory upon the town, and all the dogs of that town began to bark at the moon.

Only one dog did not bark, and he said to them in a grave voice, "Awake not stillness from her sleep, nor bring you the moon to the earth with your barking."

Then all the dogs ceased barking, in awful silence. But the dog who had spoken to them continued barking for silence, the rest of the night.

Socrates

XIII

"PITY THE NATION"

The Wanderer was given to the public in 1932, the year after Gibran's death. And in 1933 came the volume on which the poet was working up to the very day before he left this Earth, *The Garden of the Prophet*.

Gibran had originally planned for two additional volumes to complete The *Prophet* series, the one just mentioned, and the third to be called *The Death of the Prophet*. Of the last, unfortunately nothing had been written. He had talked of it often, saying, "We shall write this, and this." But only one line was written down. The line was the summing up of the tragic end that he foresaw for Almustafa. It was this: "And he shall return to the City of Orphalese . . . and they shall stone him in the market-place, even unto death; and he shall call every stone a blessed name."

It was to have been a book concerned with the relationship between man and God, even as *The Prophet* concerns relationships between man and man, and *The Garden*, between man and nature.

The Garden was, as Gibran said, "on the way." The various pieces were practically complete. No arrangement had been planned, however, and the thread of story on which the jewels of his thoughts were to be strung was missing. It was with great hesitation that I assumed the responsibility of making that arrangement and weaving that thread. And it was some time before I could bring myself to do it. But it finally became crystal clear to me that it was a privilege as well as a compulsion, something I could not get away from, day or night. There was a curious urge that came, tenuous and insistent, out of nowhere, waking me in the deep of night and questioning almost audibly, "When will you begin?"

When I did, at last, sit down to mould the book into its final form, there was no difficulty, no hesitation. The frame for the various pictures Gibran had drawn with his glowing words came into being as if he were indeed supplying the need, and so the book was finished. Many things came flowing back into my mind that I had thought forgotten, things the poet had said about *The Garden*. There were nine men who were to be with him in his mother's garden. I suddenly remembered them, but I had no memory of whom they were to be. But with perfect naturalness, as if it were a poem of my own working itself out, came the vision — three mariners from his own ship, three who had served in the Temple, and three who had been his comrades when they were but children. These were the perfect companions, and as the whole canvas began to emerge from the assembling of the pieces, I saw that it was good. These nine men took their own dramatic part in the story of Almustafa and Karima as the portions of the complete picture fell into

120

place. Their discipleship provided the reason for the words the Prophet was constrained to speak. Thus:

And on a morning his disciples sat around him, and there were distances and remembrances in his eyes. And that disciple who was called Hafiz said unto him, "Master, tell us of the City of Orphalese, and of that land wherein you tarried those twelve years."

And Almustafa was silent, and he looked away toward the hills and toward the vast ether, and there was a battle in his silence.

Then he said: "My friends and my road-fellows, pity the nation that is full of beliefs and empty of religion.

"Pity a nation that wears a cloth it does not weave, eats a bread it does not harvest, and drinks a wine that flows not from its own winepress.

"Pity the nation that acclaims the bully as hero, and that deems the glittering conqueror bountiful.

"Pity a nation that despises a passion in its dream, yet submits in its awakening.

"Pity the nation that raises not its voice save when it walks in a funeral, boasts not except among ruins, and will rebel not save when its neck is laid between the sword and the block.

"Pity the nation whose statesman is a fox, whose philosopher is a juggler, and whose art is the art of patching and mimicking.

"Pity the nation that welcomes its new ruler with

trumpetings, and farewells him with hootings, only to welcome another with trumpetings again.

"Pity the nation whose sages are dumb with years and whose strong men are yet in the cradle.

"Pity the nation divided into fragments, each fragment deeming itself a nation."

"The nine pities" Gibran called these potent pronouncements, and he spoke them with an edge on his voice that was seldom heard. Yet there is about this book a quality of extreme gentleness, of unearthly compassion, something of which Gibran has spoken in *The Prophet*, calling it "the pain of too much tenderness." Is it perhaps the foreshadowing of the separation between this green Earth and the poet who was one of the greatest lovers of the planet? He said once, "How can we conceive a heaven beyond what is spread before us here? This matchless created Earth is of the essence of God's vastest dreaming." And again, "All things that come up from the dark Earth, root, tree and branch, and every bud and berry and blade of grass, these are my children and my beloved."

And in *The Garden* we feel poignantly, this love for the dew-drop, for the snow falling, for the stone in the path of which he says, "You and the stone are one. There is a difference only in heart-beats. Your heart beats a little faster, does it, my friend? Ay, but it is not so tranquil." He had great love for "the slumbering

122

groves and the vineyards," "the streams that seek the river in the valley," "the myrtle-trees and laurel."

And on an evening Almustafa says to the nine, and to the woman Karima, "We must needs part this day." And without tarrying, save for a brief farewell word, "Almustafa went out from the Garden of his mother, and his feet were swift and they were soundless; and in a moment, like a blown leaf in a strong wind, he was far gone from them, and they saw, as it were, a pale light moving up to the heights."

And they remembered his words of farewell: "I go, but if I go with a truth not yet voiced, that very truth will again seek me and gather me, though my elements be scattered throughout the silences of eternity, and again I shall come before you that I may speak with a voice born anew out of the heart of those boundless silences . . . for God will not suffer Himself to be hidden from man, nor His word to lie covered in the abyss of the heart of man."

We hear talk from time to time about writing "by inspiration." The discussion has never been of particular interest to me. I have my own explanation of the source of the things that are given to poets to speak to the world. However, it has seemed, and still seems to me that all of the pages that had to be written into *The Garden of the Prophet* came directly from some definite and informed consciousness, and were, as Kahlil Gibran has said poetry is, "the inevitable words in the inevitable place."

Thus the book was completed. And a peace settled upon my spirit, knowing that Gibran himself had blessed the doing of his work and had sustained the worker to the end.

XIV

"I MYSELF AM A PROBLEM"

During the last years of Gibran's life there was much pressure put upon him from time to time to return to Lebanon. His countrymen there felt that he would be a great leader for his people if he could be persuaded to accept such a role. He was deeply moved by their desire to have him in their midst, but he knew that to go to Lebanon would be a grave mistake.

"I believe I could be a help to my people," he said. "I could even lead them — but they would not be lead. In their anxiety and confusion of mind they look about for some solution to their difficulties. I am not that solution. I myself am a problem. If I went to Lebanon and took the little black book [*The Prophet*], and said, 'Come let us live in this light,' their enthusiasm for me would immediately evaporate. I am not a politician, and I would not be a politician. No. I cannot fulfill their desire."

And when he received a heated letter accusing him of living a life of ease and luxury in the West and deserting his own people, he cabled in one of his rare but magnificent rages to the high official who had signed the letter, "Go you to Jahannum," and would brook no further reference to the matter. However, a few months later a small deputation from Lebanon came across six thousand miles of ocean, and besought the forgiveness of their *habibi*.

Gibran's angers were famous, but infrequent. Only an extremity of injustice or poltroonery could provoke it. But there was once a man who visited the studio uninvited, with a proposal for a business deal. Gibran listened as the man stood before him. Then his face grew black with fury. When the man ceased speaking, Gibran picked up the telephone book that lay on the table beside him. The visitor started back, thinking the book was to be turned into a weapon of attack. Instead, Gibran took the book between his two hands, tore it through the middle, and flung the pieces to the floor.

Then he shouted, "I have done this so that I should not break you in pieces! Now — get out!"

The incredible strength of the Gibran hands was a widely known legend. He said, "Before I shake the hand of my friend, I must needs take thought, so that I do not cripple him." And it was true. I have often seen some husky visitor wince and turn white at a mere handshake.

The fact that he was short in stature was always an embarrassment to him. His height was not more than five feet three or four, and he resented not being taller. But his strength of muscle and of physical endurance was legendary.

He did not, however, wish to appear more powerful

in his body than other men. He desired with all his heart to seem like "the next person." In later years, when he was no longer able to avoid the adulation and acclaim of many people, he said, "If it were not for these things I should not have become man-conscious. I was a being in the mist."

All through his life there ran a non-consciousness of the eyes and ears of the world. There was no diary betraying a desire to bequeath an ordered story of his doings, no record of the constant tribute paid to him even from his youth.

His mental world, its range and depth, was inexplicable by any standard of scholarship that we know. He could converse not only intelligently but brilliantly on any topic with any man, and exhibit a particular knowledge that even specialists in their own realms could not surpass.

But it was in the world of the spirit that Gibran truly lived his life. It was this spiritual awareness perhaps, that produced the curious effect that always accompanied his entrance into a room. When he came through a door "eternity flowed upon the air," as was once said of him. In ten minutes every other person in the room was hanging on his words. His heart was like a huge bird. Almost one could hear the beating of its wings. His lips carried laughter, but his eyes were sad with the sadness of all the world. And no wonder.

Every day of his days for many years, his high room, quiet and simple in the heart of the great city, had been the last station on the journey of a multitude of pilgrims. Little the world knew, because he did not wish it to know, that hour after hour, day after day, the feet of many sought him, eager and weary and hopeful. Many a time his own weariness exceeded the need of those who came, yet he did not turn any away. Instead he placed his hand of wisdom and compassion on the wound; he spoke a word of simple truth and the pain ceased. He was indeed the good physician to the many.

Sometimes he seemed broken with fatigue. "Their love and their sorrows are sucking my blood," he said, "and I would take up my cloak and my staff and go to a hermitage. . . . But I am not good, even to think it."

He was in truth a martyr to the faith, his faith which was to deny no man a morsel or a sip. Defeated in body, which surrendered to the unequal struggle, he was ever a conqueror in spirit. "I have the disease of work," he said. He had also the disease of generosity and selflessness.

He had intolerance only for hypocrites. All other forms of wrongdoing or misdoing he accepted either as explainable or stupid. And of all these he said, "Leave them be." But against hypocrisy he raged. The names of a certain three persons were anathema to him, and these three were women.

Gibran's acceptance of the attitude of women toward him was unique. Many women loved him with a warmth and devotion that was born of a deep gratitude and reverence, a selfless love that imposed nothing upon him and

128

sought nothing in return. Some women were in love with him. He said, "I am grateful for all love and affection. But they all think I am much better than I am. They love the poet and the painter, and would possess a bit of him. But myself — they do not see or know or love."

Discussing marriage one afternoon in the studio, after he had read the piece on *marriage* from *The Prophet*, one of the several guests said smilingly, "Tell us, why have you never married?" Smiling also he replied, "Well . . . you see it is like this. If I had a wife, and if I were painting or making poems, I should simply forget her existence for days at a time. And you know well that no loving woman would put up with such a husband for very long."

The curious one was not satisfied with the smiling answer, and prodded still deeper, "But have you never been in love?"

The change in his face was like lightning. He rose and stood, and when he spoke his voice was shaken with anger for the impertinence of the guest whom he was entertaining. Controlling himself with difficulty he said: "I will tell you a thing you may not know. The most highly sexed beings upon the planet are the creators, the poets, sculptors, painters, musicians — and so it has been from the beginning. And among them sex is a beautiful and exalted gift. Sex is always beautiful, and *it is always shy*."

He turned and walked up and down the room. Then

129

with another change of countenance and a look of pity for ignorance toward the questioner, who was, of course, a woman, he said, "As for myself, I do not know what in this world is not sex, do you? Only the little stones in the riverbed, perhaps, and the blown sands upon the shores of the great seas."

When the three guests had gone he paced for a time, his head bent, utterly oblivious of the passing moments. Then he spoke, in Arabic, a brief sentence. I could not bear to miss the thought that had come out of that stillness, so I said, "Yes — Kahlil?" He looked at me as if surprised that I was there, and there was a wistfulness like a child in both face and voice as he answered, "Silence is one of the mysteries of love."

At a memorial gathering held soon after Gibran's death, one of the distinguished American writers said, among many other things, "Of his love-life I know nothing." And indeed, how should he? Majesty neither exhibits nor discusses the communion of its sanctuary. Marriage was not for him. To live life fully with all its beauty and all its pain was Kahlil Gibran's creed. And no one who knew the richness and all-inclusiveness of this man's being could doubt that he had fulfilled his creed. No celibate has ever drunk the cup of myrrh and honey to its depth; no great lover has ever spoken of that cup when he had drunk. And it may be well affirmed that whomever he had chosen to share the cup with him would be as reticent as he.

From his youth up Gibran was a spendthrift of gra-

Gibran's Studio at 51 West Tenth Street, New York, in 1932

ciousness, and many women are adepts in their misappro-
priation of this regal coinage. Every courteous tradition
of his country flowed richly through his veins and he gave
bounteously of the warmth and devotion of close friendship. There are those who will read these pages, perhaps, whose hearts know well how inadequate words
can be.

It is always wise to be wary of the woman who appears
out of nowhere and claims a great man for her own when
he is dead. But if there be those who never say, "Lord,
Lord," but who maintain a silence, doing his works, may
it not be that these are the hands that have indeed min-
istered unto him, these the hearts that have perceived the
intricacies of his myriad being? And for myself, I do not
doubt that through the turbulent years of this man's life
the ageless and universal cry for woman-comfort went
out from his great loneliness, and that in the goodness
of God, the cry was answered. To conclude otherwise
would be the essence of stupidity.

But let us remember that the great man, dead, becomes the prey of those to whom he has reached the generous hand in some one of the various shades of friend-
liness, and who whisper of close ties that have no basis
save in their own desires. Of these he would doubtless
say, "Leave them be. They have only dreamed a dream."

Gibran talked much of what he called "spiritual chemistry," of "communion in space," by which he meant the
spiritual counterpart of physical union. He once said,
"When two people, a man and a woman, have been such

131

friends as have shared the deepest spiritual moment that life brings to human beings, they have created an entity as surely as though they had conceived and borne a child, a living, invisible force which will survive and create in its turn. They have made a song, a poem which shall not die. So — there is something in God's universe which is deathless because we are friends."

Frequently during his creative hours, he would stop in his pacing and say, almost under his breath, "There is a new whisper of life upon the firmament." He said this when he had uttered a truth of such power and beauty that his own heart was torn within him and he knew that his exquisite anguish was fully shared. "Spiritual chemistry" — rendezvous in space — a relationship possible and immeasurable and indescribable.

XV

"VIGOROUS AND FULL OF LIVING FORCE"

Gibran took always the keenest interest and delight in the life and significance of the city in which he chose to make his home. He saw, as few men see, the parallels to all ancient civilizations that are written here.

He regretted the too swift swing to machinery in every branch of manufacture and the abandonment of the old world handicrafts. Among his friends were one or two master craftsmen, oldish men with whom he talked long hours about the precious things that had been fashioned throughout the ages and were still being made in the Near East and in Europe. They agreed that something of vast value was being lost through the close and constant contact of men with machines, by way of the standardization that had descended upon this country like a plague. "One of our lovely almost forgotten words is *hand-made*," he said.

He himself had a passion for woodcarving. And he left a small number of carven figures, as perfect in technique and in expressiveness as the drawings on paper. When he was weary with everything else, exhausted and low in spirit, he worked upon these carvings, "to rest myself from myself, and from every other human being," he said.

He recoiled from the foolish extremities to which our modern architecture was running, the height of buildings and the lack of beauty and proportion in so much that was being constructed at so great a cost. He deplored the pulling down of some attractive structure because it was fifty years old, or more.

"You are like fractious children," he said. "You make your toy and play with it a while, and though it is still charming, you break it up. How do you dream that the East and Europe became so full of grandeur and of irreplaceable beauty? They built something with both heart and hand, and then they let them be!"

But he entertained great faith in the eventual integrity and nobility of this country, saying, "You are now too young and too drunk with the *gadgets* that you have achieved. You have the disease of *faster-and-bigger*. You have wandered off from the road that your great, good men have travelled. But there is an Angel that is mindful of these United States — a very mighty and stubborn Angel. He is working to make you throw away two words — *cleverness* and *publicity*. Those words are a stench in the nostrils of all angels and all gods. And remember this, he will not fail. This country will go back to the road, the road of Jefferson and Franklin, of Emerson and Whitman, and of Abraham Lincoln, the blessed."

And on another day, still with a heart aching, and yet

134

believing in the country of his adoption, he said, "Perhaps the world is a sky-garden with races and civilizations for its blossoms. Some flourish well, from others the petals fall away. Here one is withered, and beside it there is left but an empty stalk to remind us of a great red-hearted bloom. Now, on this rosebush, perhaps America is the bud just pressing at its sheath, ready to open; still hard, still green, and not yet fragrant, but vigorous and full of living force."

He perhaps never spoke a truer word, for "vigorous and full of living force" this bud, which in Gibran's brief day was getting "ready to open," has proved itself to be.

He once said, "I would like to see a modern city without street lights. The lower part of Manhattan would be as beautiful and as terrible as the Pyramids of Egypt, seen in the light of the stars and the white moon, and of no other light. What a vast gulf lies between light from the Earth and light that cometh down from above."

To the younger generation of his countrymen, those born in the West of parents who had grown up on their native soil, Gibran was one of the elect of God. They went to him in their perplexities, and he met their problems with quick understanding and divine gentleness that won their undying gratitude and devotion.

He entertained a profound belief in the power that the traditions of the Arabic world still possess in the life and thought of the young Syrian. And he wrote a message *To Young Americans of Syrian Origin* that may well be pondered by young Americans of whatever origin. This is the message:

I believe in you, and I believe in your destiny.

I believe that you are contributors to this new civilization.

I believe that you have inherited from your forefathers an ancient dream, a song, a prophecy, which you can proudly lay as a gift of gratitude upon the lap of America.

I believe that you can say to the founders of this great nation, "Here I am, a youth, a young tree whose roots were plucked from the hills of Lebanon, yet I am deeply rooted here, and I would be fruitful."

And I believe that you can say to Abraham Lincoln, the blessed, "Jesus of Nazareth touched your lips when you spoke, and guided your hand when you wrote; and I shall uphold all that you have said and all that you have written."

I believe that you can say to Emerson and Whitman and James, "In my veins runs the blood of the poets and wise men of old, and it is my desire to come to you and receive, but I shall not come with empty hands."

I believe that even as your fathers came to this land to produce riches, you were born here to produce riches by intelligence, by labor.

136

I believe that it is in you to be good citizens.

And what is it to be a good citizen?

It is to acknowledge the other person's rights before asserting your own, but always to be conscious of your own.

It is to be free in word and deed, but it is also to know that your freedom is subject to the other person's freedom.

It is to create the useful and the beautiful with your own hands, and to admire what others have created in love and with faith.

It is to produce by labor and only by labor, and to spend less than you have produced that your children may not be dependent upon the state for support when you are no more.

It is to stand before the towers of New York and Washington, Chicago and San Francisco saying in your heart, "I am the descendant of a people that builded Damascus and Byblos, and Tyre and Sidon and Antioch, and now I am here to build with you, and with a will."

It is to be proud of being an American, but it is also to be proud that your fathers and mothers came from a land upon which God laid His gracious hand and raised His messengers.

Young Americans of Syrian origin, I believe in you.

It was inevitable that this youth, being what he was and what he was destined to become, should early have seen and taken bitterly to heart the oppression of his country under the Turkish yoke. That he had seen and had fiercely resented this, even during the first dozen years of his life, became evident upon the pages of *Spirits Rebellious* — of which we have written — soon after his return to Beirut.

His later joy in the contrasting freedom of this younger generation of Syrian youth both at home and in this country, to which thousands have come, seeking, was beautiful to behold. And he was full of expectation, of the certainty of their integrity and their intelligence.

Many of these young Syrians and Lebanese have great beauty of countenance and eyes of a depth and soft darkness to be seen rather than described. They speak excellent English, but they speak it, many of them, with a lingering suggestion of the poetry and subtlety of their homeland. And they are gifted in many diverse directions.

Gibran once said, "Some of you Americans think that all we have come to this country for, from our native Syria, is to sell oranges and bananas, or rugs and brasses." But as I write there are thousands of his countrymen represented in almost all of the arts and sciences and professions in many parts of the land. There are distinguished professors in the universities; there are eminent physicians; there are brilliant musicians and composers; there

138

are poets and editors and lecturers, and there are financiers and diplomats and lawyers.

And today there are officers in our Army and our Navy and our Air Force, men in the ranks and on the home front, "young Americans of Syrian origin" who are "vigorous and full of living force."

And all of them everywhere know Gibran Kahlil Gibran as he is called in his country. They know him in the cities, in the delightful Syrian restaurants where toothsome dishes are prepared with real art and served with distinction. I have never entered one of these restaurants without hearing some mention of him, without someone knowing, and saying, "You are the friend of Gibran?" And then such lavish and ardent attention and service as they render, in his name! It is when I dine in one of these places that I am reminded how Gibran would say, emphatically, and smile, "You are Lebanese!" For there is no food that I have eaten in any country that so pleases my palate as the Syrian cuisine. Gibran himself, being as he was of simple tastes, had a menu for the perfect refreshment, "dark bread and ripe olives, Syrian cheese and white wine." And this is indeed, a satisfying and comforting repast.

And with this meal, in which he frequently indulged himself, he had the habit of weaving some little tale of beauty — "not to be written down," he said, "only to be shared." But I wish I might have kept them more clearly in my memory.

There was one tale about a crystal forest. He would

say, "We will go wandering," and then he would let his rich and vivid fancy run free. He would tell of the shining branches and the bushes heavy and glittering with frozen diamonds and pearls of ice and snow. There were great arches where the trees met overhead, and long corridors carpeted with the magic of crisp snow. There was a crystal cottage — the windows were frosted with lacy pictures, "and we may never see what is within," he said. And there was a cathedral — "but that you must see with your own inner sight, I cannot describe it," he said. "Its beauty is not of this world."

Another tale was of a cave in the rocks near the edge of the deep forest. There he would choose to wander saying, "The snow is falling." In the cave was a couch made of branches of fir and balsam piled upon the ground. There was a small fire of fagots built at the edge of the cave. "Come," he would say, "and we will sit upon the branches and beside the fire, and look out upon the forest . . . whilst the snow is falling."

And in this tale there were two snowbirds who stayed in the North Country all Winter when the other birds went South, and who sang—but only when the snow was falling. Then they would sit upon a branch, close together, on a tree close to the edge of the forest and near to the cave, and sing their song, "as the snow is falling." The phrase the tale-teller repeated over and over, almost singing it, like the refrain of a song.

The illusion was so perfect, so intense, that one would find one's self amazed, when the simple meal and the

140

quietly told tale were over, to look and see no cave and no snow and hear no birds sing. It was at these times that the shared rendezvous in space, the spiritual chemistry, the newly created entity, exercised their spell.

I understood why the poet said, "not to be written — to be shared." There was no notebook either in the crystal forest or in the cave, and one could not write down the singing of the snowbirds.

XVI

"ONCE MORE . . . IT IS FINISHED"

As I said in the beginning, it has been far from my intention to write a biography of Kahlil Gibran. Rather, I have desired to make him live for others as he lives for me, clearly and vividly as if he were in fact still upon the Earth. I have set down the story very much in the sequence in which it was lived in the years of our friendship, not in the sequence of events in his life.

But there are some things still to be said about the background of this man from Lebanon: that he was born on January 6, 1883, of Lebanese parents who lived in the little mountain village of Bsherri, four thousand years ancient, and close to the Cedars of the Lord; that his maternal grandfather, Estaphanos Rahmi, was a priest of the Maronite Church, a scholarly man, famous for his rare speaking and singing voice: that his mother was Kamila, the youngest child of this Maronite priest, his best-adored child whom he called "my heart that goes before me." We are amused to learn of the poet's paternal grandfather, who is said to have owned large estates in the north of Lebanon, that he was extremely conscious of his gifts and his importance, and had a skillful and oftentimes mortifying talent for employing the milder forms of profanity. There is a story still told of a time

142

Mary, the Mother of Jesus

when a certain Monsignor of the Church sent him a message that offended his dignity, so much so that he exploded to the messenger from His Reverence: "Tell him that Syria is the greatest province in all the Turkish Empire; that the Lebanon is the crown of Syria. Bsherri is the brightest jewel in that crown. Gibran is the most distinguished family name in Bsherri, and I am the illustrious head of that goddam family!"

Gibran told this tale with great relish, as he did also tales of his Grandmother Rahmi, who assumed in her home the prestige of the matriarch and was the acknowledged mentor of her ecclesiastical husband and their children. She bore Kamila, her last child, at the age of fifty-six, and then proceeded to live on for ten years past the century mark.

She was known as "the Regiment," and with a gallant remnant of feminine sophistry would confess to only one hundred and six years. After her eightieth year she crossed the Lebanon range on horseback, and she retained all of her keenness and her assumption of authority to the very end of her days. When she was very old she once said to Gibran, "I have left all of my silver to my other grandson, so that he may not hate you!"

On one occasion when Gibran returned from Al-Hikmat to Bsherri bearing certain honours and prizes, "the Regiment" sat with Grandmother Gibran discussing the lad's gifts and graces of person and character. The latter said gently, as was her wont, "We are proud indeed of his rare talents and genius." To which the other shouted,

"And what have you to do with it? He is my grandson!"

And when a gathering of the branches of the family was arranged in honour of her one hundredth birthday, so many generations were represented that a small child being sent to summon one of the guests to the presence of "the Regiment," said, "Grandmother, your Grandmother wants to see you."

The youngest daughter, Kamila, was a widow with a small son, Peter, when Khalil Gibran, several years her senior, heard her singing in her father's garden. He did not rest until he had met her, and he was immediately possessed with her beauty and charm. And there was no peace for him or anyone else until he had won her hand.

The first child of their union was named for the father, Khalil, which spelling the poet changed later to Kahlil, the one that he preferred. The name means "the chosen, the beloved friend," even as Kamila means "the perfect," and Gibran "the healer or comforter of souls." The Arabic name has always a definite significance.

Kamila Gibran had several languages to her credit, which accounts somewhat for her son's linguistic affluence. She had inherited from her father, the beloved priest, a wonderful singing voice; the strange haunting songs of that Eastern world, as her fingers touched the strings of the *oud*, were among the small Kahlil's earliest joys. He told how she would sing to him in the dusk "until the stars began to hang down." For it is true that in the night sky above Lebanon the stars do seem as though they are pendent, swinging from the depths of blue above. When one visits that mountain village they say, "If you will lie on the housetop to sleep, you may reach up and pluck a star and put it under your pillow."

So Kamila Gibran sang to her little son both the ancient songs and songs of her own that were not written down. She would weave for him the old tales of Haroun-al-Raschid and all the Arabic wonderland. To her it was given early in the pattern of the years to comprehend what manner of child had been born to her. And she said somewhat later, "My son is outside of psychology," for he was unpredictable and difficult, tender over a broken flower at one moment, and the next raging like a young lion because of some imposing of authority upon him. He said over and over again, "I was really not a nice boy, but it was because I was restless. I felt strange and lost. I could not find my way. But my mother knew it, though I never told her. I did not need to tell her."

It was true. She had watched him from the early days when he had sat brooding for hours over the book of Leonardo. She had stood by to quiet his small fury when something did not please him. And it was she, against the will and wish of her own heart, but trusting his will and wisdom, who had overcome all the objections when he had insisted upon having his education in Lebanon.

During the last weeks of his life he talked constantly of his youth, of his mother and of his sister Marianna, the only one of their family left to him. Of Marianna he said, "If there is a saint living upon this Earth it is Marianna Gibran, the daughter of my Mother."

145

I believe that he knew full well that he was about to leave this life, though he never spoke of it. But on one evening, not many weeks before that April tenth, he seemed weighed down with an unendurable sadness, and I asked, "What is it? What has happened to make you so sad?" He was silent for what seemed a long time. Then he said, "There is something I want you to know, yet I do not want to tell you. . . . Can you think what it might be?" He asked it thus because so often the one knew quite well what the other was thinking, without words.

Yet on this occasion I had no inkling of what was in his mind. When I left the studio that evening he said, "If you do think what it is — that I want you to know, will you tell me?" I promised and went away torturing myself trying to think what it might be, but with no success. Long afterward, after he was gone, it came to me that his lonely human heart wanted to share the certainty of approaching death, but that he would not sadden me with the tidings if I did not read them for myself. And I feel that it was best so. If I had known, it would have been difficult for the heart to keep singing, as we did keep singing during those final days.

They were days of almost feverish work, completing several of the latest wash-drawings to be published in *The Wanderer*. He was using a new combination of hues, shades of sepia with shades of white, resulting in compositions of startling beauty — the drawings of *Joy*

146

and Sorrow, The Dancer, and the tall mystical figure of the woman, which he called *Like unto Eternity.* These were barely finished before the dawn of Good Friday.

It was the poet's custom to spend that day alone, in complete solitude. Then, when twilight drew on and the hour of acute remembrance of the Crucifixion had passed, he would call on the phone and say, "Once more . . . it is finished." This he did on that last Good Friday.

On Easter Sunday he was at work again, saying, "I have the disease of work!"

And that disease consumed him. He was literally devoured by the flame of his tireless passion, which encompassed the fagots of his body. And it was truly a fire whose scorching was terrible as the furnace heated seven times. Again and again in moments of extreme creation he cried out, "I burn!" not knowing that he had cried out at all.

It was on that Easter Sunday, five days before he left this good green Earth, that he said with quiet authority, "I know my destiny." And that he had long known it is beyond the peradventure of a doubt.

There have been many who have bitterly resented his early passage to the Unknown, saying, "His work was not yet done." But he himself had said, "I know that I shall not leave this strangely beautiful Earth until the angels see that my work is finished. And I feel that the 'I' in me will not perish, it will not be drowned in the great sea that is called God."

147

And let it not be supposed for a single moment that the man who was given the power to perceive human need and to minister to it in so full a measure was not given also the consciousness of his anointment. He had long known what was his to perform and to endure, and he did both with a blending of boldness and gentleness, sparing all who were dear and close to him all that was possible of the stupendous knowledge. He gave utterance to startling truth that seemed to brush away the smug pretense of this cocksure latter day. And he dismissed the anxieties of the present with a word, "We have Eternity."

Often the poet prefaced some unforgettable expression of desire with the words, "If I should die tonight —" And on one evening the wish of his heart was this: "Remember that one of my dearest dreams is this dream, that sometime, somewhere a body of work, perhaps fifty or seventy-five paintings shall be hung together in a gallery of some institution in a large city where people may see them, and perhaps love them."

In *The Garden of the Prophet* this man from Lebanon has left a simple and profound profession of faith concerning that which lies beyond the door that we call Death:

I shall live beyond death, and I shall sing in your ears
Even after the vast sea-wave carries me back
To the vast sea-depth.
I shall sit at your board though without a body,

148

And I shall go with you to your fields, a spirit invisible.
I shall come to you at your fireside, a guest unseen.
Death changes nothing but the masks that cover our
    faces.
The woodsman shall be still a woodsman,
The ploughman, a ploughman.
And he who gave his song to the wind shall sing it
    also to the moving spheres.

Nearness to this planet that he so loved, continuity
of the treasures of the spirit, these things were in his
vision. For he said, "I long for Eternity, for there I
shall meet my unwritten poems and my unpainted pictures."

In ceaseless measure Gibran Kahlil Gibran had given
himself to the world, and this deep and deathless love
shall be ever "his honour and his reward." From the
very summit of his years he stepped forth saying, with
majesty and wisdom undiminished, "Now, I will rise
and strip me of time and space."

And from his *Earth Gods* we take the final chant:

My god-heart within my human ribs
Shouts to my god-heart in mid-air.
The human pit that wearied me calls to divinity.
The beauty that we have sought from the beginning
Calls unto divinity.
I heed, and I have measured the call,
And now I yield.

149

Beauty is a path that leads to self self-slain.
Beat your strings.
I will to walk the path.
It stretches ever to another dawn.

It was on April tenth, at eleven o'clock in the evening, the first Friday after Easter of 1931 that Kahlil Gibran went into the sky. He had said to me, "Stay with me. Don't leave me. . . . All is well." And his actual going, after hours of perfect silence, was no more than one long, deep-drawn breath, a great breath as though an invisible bird had escaped at last into the ecstasy of freedom and flight.

XVII

"READY AM I TO GO"

Come for leave-taking, O sons of my mother.
Bring now the children with their finger-tips
    of lily and of rose.
Let the aged come to bless my forehead with
    their withered hands,
And call the daughters of the meadow and
    the field,
That they may behold the shadows of the
    unknown pass beneath my brows,
And hear in my last breath the echo of infinity.
Lo, I have reached the summit;
I have outstripped the cries of men,
And I hear naught save the vast hymn of
    this eternity.*

In New York City and in Boston, his first home in
America, thousands of human beings gave evidence that
the "I" in Gibran will not "perish from the Earth." For
two days and the intervening night the sleeper lay in
state in the latter city with a guard of honour, young men
from his own home town, attending throughout the

* From an unpublished poem by Kahlil Gibran.

hours. An endless stream of sorrowing humanity passed silently before the quiet form of their *habibi*, and the word was murmured between sobs, by young and old. Many of these mourners were people from his own country. And sitting not far away in a shadowed corner, it seemed to the onlooker that it was all taking place at another time and in a distant place, for among the multitude might be seen one who was the counterpart of what Peter had been, or John, the beloved disciple, or a bearded old hermit or a wanderer from the desert, so definitely had these people retained their native personalities. Many a one dropped upon his knees and sobbed aloud, and the young guard of honour, with tears overflowing, stood immovable.

It will always be a strange phenomenon to me that through all this length of days when the observances and the rituals of the ancient Maronite faith were being solemnized, there was so little of personal grief or bereavement within my heart. Never to be forgotten was the wonder of it, the complete abandonment of anguish of these people, the beauty of their faces, a tragic beauty, and the words they spoke to me about this loving man lying silent before them.

It was as though myself were saying to myself, "He is their own. He belongs to them. You were given the gift of his friendship for a brief space, but he is of the very fabric of their breath and being. Stand away, and leave him to their loving and their brokenhearted tenderness."

152

In the little Church of our Lady of the Cedars there was a service; there was the priest, the Right Reverend Monsignor Stephen Douaihy, a close and devoted friend of the poet for many years, who conducted the ancient funeral rites in Syriac. There was the young acolyte, swinging the censor, and the young Syrian girl singing in his native tongue an old-country chant that Gibran had often heard her sing.

The tiny church was crowded to the doors, and grief was everywhere evident in that place. Outside were hundreds who could not gain admission. And when the service was over, we who passed out between the waiting crowds saw a sight seldom seen in any Western city. Hundreds of people dropped upon their knees, on the sidewalks, in the street, and there was a sound of low, hardly controlled weeping that was almost unearthly in its rhythm.

The people rose and followed the cortege, and in the great city of Boston the traffic was halted for twenty minutes along the line that was taken to the temporary resting-place for this man from Lebanon.

Weeks later the silent homeward journey of Gibran Kahlil Gibran was begun. Following a dawn veiled with the mist that he loved so well, his body was borne from the tomb in Boston to the pier in Providence, there to embark for the last time upon any earthly pilgrimage. Through the gentle gray rain a long line of cars drove westward in the early morning to take farewell of the

153

poet-painter and his sister Marianna, who was making the journey with her beloved to Beirut and Bsherri.

And one who had known so well his passion for the rain and the snow and for "all that comes down from the sky" could but remember how he had said a thousand times, when the wind and the tempests beset his high window, "How I thank God for this! It releases something in me!" And it seemed fitting that rain should fall now, when all that had been within him was released.

Again at Providence the great crowds of those who had come to pay their homage of love and sorrow thronged the pier. And there were quiet words of pride and grief spoken above the casket that was draped with the flags of the United States and of the Lebanon.

Finally, a portion of *The Prophet*, the words of Almustafa where he says:

> Sons of my ancient mother, you riders of the tides,
> How often have you sailed in my dreams. And now
> you come in my awakening which is my deeper dream.
> Ready am I to go, and my eagerness with sails full
> set awaits the wind.

It was then that Monsignor Douaihy pronounced a final word of benediction and farewell, and the casket, with the two flags that this man had loved, was lowered into the ship while the wind instruments played the *Pilgrims' Chorus* from *Tannhäuser*, *Asa's Death* from *Peer Gynt*, and *Nearer, My God, to Thee*.

The ship put out from the pier, and the earthly chap-

Jeanne d'Arc

ter of a great life in this Western land of steel and stone
came to an end, leaving a silence and an emptiness in the
hearts and the places that had known him and should
know him no more, but leaving also a living memory of
his own words:

> Fare you well, People of Orphalese.
> This day has ended.
> What was given us here we shall keep,
> And if it suffices not, then again must we come to-
> gether and together stretch our hands unto the giver.
> Forget not that I shall come back to you.
> A little while, and my longing shall gather dust and
> foam for another body.
> A little while, a moment of rest upon the wind, and
> another woman shall bear me.

And his own country, Lebanon, from the moment that
the ship dropped anchor in the beautiful harbor of Saint
Georges at Beirut, added a testimony of tribute and pride
that has not been known before "in the hoary history of
Lebanon." The Arabic press bears witness that never
has such homage been paid to any man, living or dead.
From far and near the throngs of the grieving came
to their capital city, and even from beyond the bounds
of Lebanon itself, from the greater Syria. For the bells
had tolled the tidings all up and down that land, the tidings of the death of this man from Lebanon who had
achieved the height of their most ardent dreams, and on
that day of his passing their greatest sorrow had been

155

born. From ancient Damascus, from Homs and Hama, from Antioch and Sidon and Tripoli they came, and from the Holy Land to the south, to do honour to their dead.

Officially reported in the *Syrian World*, we find these words:

> The body was received with official pomp and ceremony. Government representatives in official dress were present at the pier, with priests and high dignitaries of the Church in their clerical robes, and a multitude of just plain people who were nearest and dearest to the heart of the dead poet.
>
> Thence the body was carried to the Maronite Cathedral of Saint Georges, where the Right Reverend Ignatius Mobarak, Maronite Archbishop of Beirut, and his clergy, received the body with the chanting of Syriac lamentations.
>
> Especially prominent, in their picturesque native dress, and the expression of deep sorrow on their proud faces, were the men and women who had come down from Bsherri in northern Lebanon.

The President of Lebanon with his ministers, members of the High French Commissariat, and ranking officers of the French Admiralty attended upon this silent man, and "all differences, social, political, and religious were forgotten." Christians, Mohammedans, and Jews left the mission and the mosque and the synagogue to stand beside his bier, and little children came by the hundreds because they had learned to know and love the name of Gibran.

Most moving was the journey along the coastal route from Beirut to Tripoli and up the mountain, for from every town and village and hamlet the people came forth and met him upon the road. The young men, in an ancient form of tribute to a dead warrior, engaged in swordplay before the slowly moving hearse; the poets and the women chanted elegy and lamentation as they came beating their breasts in rhythm with their chanting. As the funeral cortege drew near to Gebail, the ancient Byblos, which was the shrine of the Syrian goddess Astarte, a company of maidens with white robes and flowing hair strewed roses upon the roadway, and sang in welcome to the homecoming, but they sang as though "the beautiful bridegroom of dreams" were living and not dead, and they scattered perfume with the roses and upon the casket.

Thus, in a fashion that may seem pagan and ornate to the Western mind, did the most loyal and most loving people in the world betoken their sorrow as their forefathers had done for centuries.

And now, in Bsherri, half a world away, near the Cedars of the Lord, the body of Gibran is lying, Gibran, our friend and brother, he who is more than any other the poet of the Cedars. And there the Bsherrians, both those who remain in the mountain town and the many who have gone out into the lands of all the Earth, will

157

erect a tomb as sanctuary for the body of their countryman, and there will arise also a memorial in stainless
marble, conceived and executed by the only living Lebanese sculptor, Yusef Hoyiek, who was Gibran's close
friend in their youth when they were students together
at Al-Hikmat. The figures in the memorial will immor-
talize in stone some of the dreams that Gibran has left on
paper and on canvas; and they are even now coming into
being under the sculptor's hand.

XVIII

"PEACE BE WITH YOU"

There remain but a few threads to be caught up into this weaving of the story. One book that was published three years after Gibran's death, a book called *Prose Poems*, holds, I believe, a special interest for those who care to look deeply into the origins of the poet's legacy of the written word. This book is entirely a translation from poems written in Arabic during his early years and taken from one or another of the volumes of Arabic poems. We owe our gratitude for this volume to the devoted and untiring work of a young countryman of Gibran's whose appreciation and understanding of the originals has resulted in a splendid reproduction of twelve early prose poems. This young man is Andrew Ghareeb, and through this labour of love he has given us the only volume of work thus translated. Mr. Ghareeb was a frequent visitor to the poet's studio, and had Gibran's permission to undertake the difficult task of rendering into English the magic of the original Arabic. The difficult task has been well done.

The general comment that I have heard concerning this book has been that it is "different." Readers say, "It doesn't seem exactly like Gibran." Yet they are wrong.

It must seem like Gibran, for it is the very essence of Gibran. It is his young self who speaks throughout the book. Here he has not, as in later volumes, put words into the mouths of others.

He says, "*I* purified my lips with the sacred fire to speak of love." He says, "It was but yesterday that *I* stood at the door of the temple." He says, "*I* beheld three figures sitting upon a rock," and he says, "My soul counselled me, my brother, and enlightened me." And still again he says:

> On the day that my mother gave me birth,
> On that day five-and-twenty years ago,
> Silence placed me in the vast hands of life,
>   abounding with struggle and conflict.

In the same poem upon his birthday:

> Mankind have I loved. Ay, much have I
>   loved men,
> And men in my opinion are three:
> The one who curses life, the one who
>   blesses it, and the one who
>   contemplates it.
> The first I have loved for his misery, the
>   second for his beneficence, and the
>   third for his wisdom.

And at the close of the poem we find a litany for peace that is classic in its music and beauty. It contains these lines:

160

Peace be with you, years, which disclose what
    the years have hidden!
Peace be with you, ages, which restore what
    the centuries have destroyed!
Peace be with you, time, which moves with us
    unto the perfect day!

To be sure this is not *The Prophet* nor *Jesus, The Son of Man* nor any of the other several pronouncements, but it is Gibran, warp and woof. And I have heard him read these very words, translating freely from his own Arabic, and I say to you that there is nothing in all the English books that is one whit more the very essence of the poet than these words. Perhaps if the translation had been Gibran's own there might have been a touch that we miss. I have said, and I believe it to be true, that no one can or will ever translate the Gibran Arabic into the Gibran English as the poet himself could have done. But he would not translate. It will be only through the devoted labour of one who knows both languages that we shall ever be able to unlock all the treasure that remains hidden to this day.

In the *Introduction* to the *Prose Poems*, which I was privileged to write, I have said:

Perhaps some small measure of the heat from that deep fire of which the original poems were the flame may be felt herein; perhaps some rushlight of the poet's profound realization — the tragic beauty and rightness of life, and the supreme assurance that "We have eternity" — may be found and followed; perhaps there may beat through the succeeding rhythms some echo of the poet's own heart-beat. That these things may be so is the hope of Andrew Ghareeb and myself.

Reading the slight volume through again, at this time, I am shaken anew by the power and beauty of all that it declares and all that it intimates. *Prose Poems* is a book that Gibran would applaud modestly, as he did one or another of the little black books, saying, "Well, I think we may say that it is a good little book."

I have said that the hypocrite was the only doer of wrong whom Gibran excluded from his understanding and his forgiveness. His compassion extended to all others, no matter what their sin. In a prose poem written when the poet was still in his early teens and was just beginning to try his command of English, he expressed with a childlike naïveté this acceptance of those who had "made a wrong turning," as he said. Reading this aloud one evening, he mused over it — an old yellowed paper, torn at the edges — and he said, "Yes . . . some day we shall whip this, and then it will do." It was never whipped, that is, pondered over, and pruned here and there, a word taken out, a word put in, as he was wont to do with any bit of writing from his "green youth." The poem I shall give you exactly as that "green youth" conceived it, and in my opinion still "it will do." Such di-

162

vine compassion and tenderness is a revelation of the
spirit of this man, from his youth up.

Jesus Knocking at the Gate of Heaven.

Father, my Father, open Your gate!
I bring with me a goodly company.
Open the gate that we may come in.
We are the children of Your heart, each one and all.
Open, my Father, open Your gate.

Father, my Father, I knock at Your gate.
I bring a thief who was crucified with me
  this very day.
In spite of this
He is a gentle soul, and he would be Your guest.
He thieved a loaf for his children's hunger.
But I know the light in his eyes would gladden You.

Father, my Father, open Your gate.
I bring a woman who gave herself to loving,
And they raised stones against her,
But knowing Your deeper heart, I held them back.
The violets are not withered in her eyes,
And Your April is yet upon her lips.
Her hands still hold the harvest of Your days,
And now she would enter with me to Your house.

Father, my Father, open the gate.
I bring to You a murderer,

A man with twilight on his face.
He hunted, for his young,
But unwisely did he hunt.
The warmth of the sun was upon his arms,
The sap of Your Earth was in his veins;
And he desired meat for his kin
Where meat was denied,
But his bow and arrow were too ready,
And he committed murder.
And for this he is now with me.

Father, my Father, open Your gate.
I bring with me a drunkard,
A man who thirsted for other than this world.
It was his to sit at Your board, with a cup,
With loneliness at his right hand,
And at his left hand desolation.
He gazed deep into the cup
And therein he saw Your stars mirrored
        in the wine,
And he drank deep for he would reach Your sky.

He would reach his greater self,
But he was lost upon the way, and he fell down.
I raised him, Father, from outside the Inn,
And he came with me, laughing half the way.
Now, though in my company, he weeps,
For kindness hurts him.
And for this I bring him to Your gate.

Father, my Father, open the gate.
I bring with me a gambler,
A man who would turn his silver spoon into
    a golden sun;
And like one of Your spiders
Would weave the web and wait
For the fly that was also hunting the
    smaller flies.
But he lost like all gamblers,
And when I found him wandering the streets
    of the city
I looked into his eyes,
And I knew that his silver turned not into
    gold,
And the thread of his dreams was broken.
And I bade him to my company.
I said to him "Behold your brothers' faces
And My face.
Come with us, we are going to the fertile land be-
    beyond the hills of life.
Come with us."
And he came.

Father, my Father, You have opened the gate!
Behold, my friends.
I have sought them far and near;
But they were in fear and would not come with me
Until I revealed to them Your promise and
    Your grace.

Now, that you have opened Your gate
And received and welcomed my companions,
There are on Earth no sinners,
Shut away from You and Your receiving.
There is neither hell nor purgatory;
Only You and heaven exist, and upon Earth, Man,
The son of Your ancient heart.

This was Gibran.

The many-sidedness of Kahlil Gibran is clearly evident throughout all his works. And there are many bits of expression, found and cherished on small pieces of paper, that are like highlights on the tapestry of his story. In telling of camping out in the Lebanon with other youths during his college days, he said, "When I sleep out of doors under the stars, one of my friends will say, 'How high are you?' And I will say, if I am very sleepy, 'Very . . . high' . . . in a drowsy voice. And if I am not so sleepy I will shout back, 'Oh, not so high.' And sometimes someone will say, 'How far, now, madman?' And I will not answer, . . . I am so high."

And again: "The strange beauty of the desert! If you hear a flute upon the night, you turn to me and say, 'Kahlil, are you playing the flute?' And I answer you, 'No — that is someone fifteen, seventeen miles away.' The night is so still, the stars are so close."

And many other things he said, rich in quality and beauty as these which follow:

I have told you how, when I was a child, we went — every human being in the village — on the Eve of Christmas to the church, walking through the deep silent snow, and bearing, each one, his lighted lantern through the night, and how at the moment of midnight the bells and the voices of old men and children raised an ancient chant of Galilee, and the roof of the little church seemed to me to open unto the sky. In that very church, today, there is a reading-desk that was carved by my cousin N'Oula, the same N'Oula who is now the father of my godchild, the little Kahlil. I should like to see that desk again and listen to its silent word.

I have been thinking today of the Grandmother of Jesus, and of her pride in him. . . . Can you not see her, bearing Him with love and joy, up to the roof-top at eventide to show Him to the evening star? And as he grew can you not see her, with a smile of love upon her lips, raising her finger at Him in mild rebuke? For though He was a child like other children yet His ways were wise and old, and He was not obedient unto the misjudgment of women.

If you and I should speak nothing but stark truth for five minutes all our friends would abandon us; if for ten minutes, we would be exiled from the land; if for fifteen minutes, we would be hanged!

I believe that there are groups of people and individuals the world over who are kin regardless of race. They are in the same realm of consciousness. This is kinship, only this.

When I was born I said, "I will go back." When I was three years old a tempest visited Bsherri, and I tore my clothes and shouted, "I go with the storm!" At twelve I said, "I will stay here awhile for I have something to say." At twenty I had forgotten what to say. At thirty-three I began to remember.

If there were only one star in the firmament, one flower forever in white bloom, and one tree arising from the plain; and if the snow should fall but once in every hundred years, then we would know the generosity of the infinite.

Create Beauty and let every other thing go to hell!

Various opinions of art and poetry were expressed by Gibran in writing at one time or another.

I believe that the art of today owes its best elements to the Arabs who kept and cherished the spirit in which the Book of the Dead, The Avista, the Book of Job, and the Chaldean man-headed winged bull were written and carved. By the art of today I mean that almost religious hunger not yet a century old, which is the

168

golden link between the man of today and the greater man of tomorrow. . . . The Greek artist had a keener eye and a cleverer hand than the Chaldean or the Egyptian, but he did not possess that third Eye which they both possessed. Greece borrowed her gods from Chaldea, Phoenicia, and Egypt. She borrowed every quality save that vision, that insight, that peculiar consciousness of what is deeper than depth and higher than height. She brought from Byblos and Nieth the jug and the cup, but not the wine. She was capable of fashioning the naively formed jug and cup into golden vessels, but she never filled them with aught but liquid realism.

To me the only mighty being in the Greek mythology is Prometheus, but let us not forget that the original fire-bringer is Chaldean and not Greek. The races of Western Asia knew him two thousand years before the Trojan expedition.

There are few people in this world who love Greek art as much as I, but I love it for what it is, not for what it is not. I love the charm, the freshness, the loveliness, the physical glory of all things Grecian, but I cannot find in these the living God. I see only a shadow of His shadow."

A comment on literature:

The greatest literatures are probably the Arabic, or rather the Semitic — for I include the Hebrew — the Greek and the English. . . . Genius is a protest against things as they seem to exist. Keats and Shelley were protests. They loved the English scene, but they gave it a classic setting in an imaginary world. So did Spenser.

But the Greeks and the Romans were at home with the Greek and the Roman world; they were less like aliens. The French, too, are at home. They accept. Dante did not. He was the greatest of all protests.

And again of Shelley:

He is a world in himself. His soul is that of an excited god who, being sad and weary and homesick, passed the time singing of other worlds. He is in a way the least English of the English poets, and the most Oriental from an Oriental point of view.

And last from a letter written from Boston, a few weeks before the sudden beginning of the writing of *Jesus:*

Last night I saw his face again, clearer than I have ever seen it. It was not turned toward my face — it was looking far out into the vast night. I saw the profile. It was at once serene and stern, and I thought for a moment that he would smile, but he did not. He was youth, ageless and immortal; not God, no, but the Son of Man, facing all that man must face, knowing all that man has ever known, or shall ever know. His was the face of one invincible. It was the face of a lover and a brother and a friend. His hair was blown back

Last Photograph of Gibran

from his face, and like unto small shining wings each side his head. His throat was brown and strong, his eyes were like dark embers. Now, my friend, for the first time I feel sure that I can draw that face. It shall be like the figurehead for the prow of a great ship.

He walked as a man facing into a strong wind, yet who was stronger than the wind. He wore again the rough woolen garment, and again his feet were bare and dusty from the curving roads. I saw again his firm large hands and stalwart wrists, like branches of a tree. His head was high, and upon his countenance I beheld a vast purpose and a silent yearning.

XIX

"WE HAVE ETERNITY"

To visit the Wadi Qâdisha, the valley of the Holy River, is to leave the modern world and to be plunged body and spirit into an atmosphere both ancient and timeless. The ravines and chasms cut by this river possess a drama that takes one's breath and one's words.

To reach this region of legend and parable, we drove along the coastal route from Beirut toward Tripoli, over perfect macadam roads, passing miles of banana, tobacco, and sugar cane plantations, small, beautifully tended orchards of figs and olives, of apricots, oranges, and mulberry. There is a wide strip of fertile land between the mountains and the sea, and every foot is turned to advantage by the picturesque but none the less thrifty and hard-working Lebanese.

We passed flocks of the fat-tailed sheep, and their shepherds, looking as they must have looked in the ancient days. Then we turned — after going through Gebail, the ancient Byblos, and took the mountain road that leads to the *arz er rubb*, Cedars of God, and to Bsherri, almost in the shadow of those venerable giants of the forest.

In the depth of the valley from which we began the

172

climb of about nine thousand feet, it is green and fertile and glorious with trees. Here the river is met by many mountain streams, which rush down from the springs and snows above. As we ascend the craggy heights they become stony and bare of verdure for the most part, with only a scattering of the smallish cedars, here and there. But the majestic beauty of these mountain contours is as unforgettable as it is indescribable.

The highest heights are gray and secret and implacable until they grow tender and exquisite with rose and violet and golden light as one sees them at dawn or at sunset. It is beauty of a wild and unbridled quality, and it has a mighty force that compels the mind to dwell upon the words "We have eternity."

Here time and the pressure of events seem to have receded into a vague distance. Not miles, but ages, seem to have intervened between that city of Beirut, teeming with noise, colour, and bustling life, and these mountain fastnesses with their silence, their hermits who live, solitary devotees, in caves immured in their contemplation of things eternal, and their shepherds, motionless beside their sheep.

Here we begin to envision something of the magic of this man from Lebanon. This is his home, these things are in his spirit, and of this beauty he is the child and the lover. We lose all sense of the imminence of war even though we have just passed by the armed camps of the hurriedly mobilized soldiery (for it is October of nineteen thirty-nine). We forget that Beirut and Damascus are cities blacked out at night, the streets thronged with French territorial troops, the huge Senegalese brought in for fear of an enemy attempt upon the little Republic of Lebanon, which has no army, no navy, and only the wholly inadequate gendarmerie for its protection.

We go on toward Bsherri. Gibran Kahlil Gibran, we say to ourselves. . . . And we climb and climb, the air growing rarer. We begin to feel the altitude, but we are exhilarated rather than disturbed. The road is like a shining, twisting serpent.

We pass through a village, and the friends who are making the pilgrimage with us tell us the name of the village. These friends are courteous and gracious and distinguished Lebanese — the Curator of the National Museum at Beirut, one of the foremost journalists of the Lebanon, a member of the High French Commission, and a young science professor from the American University. They are our friends because of Gibran, and their devotion to him and to his memory warms the hearts that have traveled six thousand miles to this homeland of Gibran.

Another village, and another. Buildings the colour of old ivory, with rust-red roofs. Again and again the shepherd with his little flock grazing upon a bit of green on the mountainside. The people look at us as we drive slowly through looking at them. They have beautiful eyes and warm, wide smiles, and their clothing is not

174

like our clothing. It belongs to that older simpler civilization, and we like it.

Our friends say, "They know who you are. They have heard that the American friend of Gibran will visit the Monastery today. That is why they are all out watching. You must smile at them and wave your hand." We do so, but we can hardly see their faces now, for the thought of their great love for their poet of the Cedars brings sudden tears.

The road that he had traveled, many times. The villages he knew so well. The very people, the older ones, who had heard him and seen him in his boyhood. . . .

And all the way the terraces of grapevines, with their rich and luscious harvest already being gathered, miles and miles of these terraces, beautiful in their order and pattern.

We have come far beyond and above any reminder of what is going on back there in the cities or in the outer world. We are in a world close to the sky, so it seems, and we look still higher and higher where the snow lies upon the very summit of the Lebanons, always lying there, silent and pure in outline, and secret as God Himself.

Then — we have arrived at Bsherri.

In the Chapel of the Monastery of Mar-Sarkis there is a little crypt where they have laid him. To this place many pilgrimages are made. Many silent people stand or kneel before the casket, which rests upon its carven bier. There the candles are burned and the prayers are said, prayers by persons of many faiths, for Gibran was spiritual brother to all men, and they know it, and no creed or cult or colour stands between.

The Monastery is very old. No one seems to know quite how old it really is. It is rugged and dark-hewn out of the very side of the mountain. Some of its chambers have the actual rock of the mountain for their walls. It is a place Gibran loved and frequented in his youth, and it was his wish to go back and live for a time in this very place. It is surrounded by the Cedars that he loved. But his wish was also that he might lie in the "good dark Earth." And I think his free spirit hovers near the spot hoping to see the discarded garment of his humanity sometime lowered into the quiet solitude of the waiting soil.

In a modest little building in Bsherri, taken over for the purpose, we found the considerable number of drawings and paintings — about seven hundred and fifty — and the beloved furnishings that the poet had used for years in his New York studio. Here are the chair in which he sat and the table whereupon he laid the brown notebooks and wrote the words of *The Prophet* five times over.

Here the great oils hang upon the low walls, and the drawings of *The Great Mother*, *The Sacrifice*, *Earth Gods*, *The Tree of Life*, as well as literally hundreds of other, but no less beautiful, pencil drawings, lie upon the long tables in portfolios that the painter had handled many times while he was yet here.

It is the wish of many that these priceless treasures shall be removed to Beirut and placed in an appropriate memorial museum to be devoted solely to the work of Gibran. I learned that a distinguished Lebanese has offered to present to the city a fine plot of ground upon which to erect the museum that they visualize for the reception of the Gibran collection.

The war has, of course, halted whatever may have been contemplated in this connection, but it is devoutly to be hoped that such a wise and fitting consummation may come to pass when peace is once more upon the little country and the great world.

Coming down from the mountains some time later, we drove in wonder through the glory and beauty of the Lebanese night. As daylight faded, the heights of the Lebanon Range became a bewilderment of breathtaking splendour, purple and amethyst and sapphire like the waters of the Mediterranean. As the dusk advanced the sky paled to rose and soft azure and silver, and the mountains under the sudden myriads of stars gleamed darkly beautiful like polished bronze and ebony. It was a night such as one sees in a dream, seldom in reality.

Down, down the mountain road to the coastal city of Tripoli, through its blacked-out streets, its dull blue lights showing shrouded and dim from the door and window of bazaar and Inn, while strange music like the sound of a crying voice floated on the air. It was an Arabic song accompanied by the *oud*, and throughout the city as we crept in and out of the careful traffic, we heard it, the half-sad, half-wild strains played by groups of Lebanese — Christians and Mohammedans — gathered in gardens and on balconies, singing into the night, there being little else to do in the unlighted city.

As we continued our way along the seacoast and into Beirut I could not but remember Gibran's saying about the modern city without lights. And here was this once radiant city of his own land lighted now, just as he had wished, by the light of the moon and stars only, for the tiny occasional blue bulbs along the streets seemed no more than fireflies in a dusk. But he would not have wished this to be for the reason that the beloved small country had become an armed camp, though he had entertained a definite foresight of the debacle that threatened.

This Beirut was not the Beirut of his day. To the usual riot of colour and variety of costume were added uniforms of every description. One jostled soldiers on every street and in every tram. Hotel lobbies and dining rooms were filled with officers, and the hotels themselves, the luxurious modern Saint Georges, the Metropole, the quaint and delightful Pension Saint Charles (where I had at last comfortably settled myself hopefully for the length of my stay) wholesomely presided over by German nuns — all were taken over by the mili-

178

tary. The state government was liquidated and the President of the Republic became a figurehead with a small group of official associates. The world was at war, and little Lebanon, a French mandate, was caught firmly in the toils.

And what, you ask, has all this to do with the seven years of friendship of which I write? Just this, that, the war hysteria notwithstanding, everywhere I went the name of the poet was like a distinguished-service medal pinned on my breast.

From the moment when the *Excalibur* was preparing to land and the official examination of passports was under way — they questioned me severely when they saw the word *Writer* — one word was my talisman.

"What are you going to write?" in an accusing tone.

"A book about a Lebanese poet and painter."

"What is his name?" still with suspicion.

"Gibran."

"Gibran Kahlil Gibran?"

"Yes."

It was sufficient. I was not detained one instant longer. Everyone, everywhere knew of him. And the word somehow spread very rapidly that there was someone in Beirut from America, a friend of Gibran. And I found that the whole city was my friend, in his name and for his sake.

Men of distinction and prominence who had been college-mates of the poet came to my hotel to talk of him, and to ask many questions about his life in America, among them the commandant of the gendarmerie of Lebanon, Colonel Elias Midawwer, who has recently won additional honors by reason of his stand in the cause of the Allies.

At length the day of sailing was imminent. All Americans who were not residents of the country were being urged upon their homeward way. But there was one more visit to be made.

On the site of the old Madrasat Al-Hikmat a handsome modern structure has been erected, as perfect an educational institution as can be conceived. On the last Sunday of our sojourn in the Lebanon it was there I went with my little four-year-old grandson Christopher, who had accompanied me like the trooper that he is, through all the long weeks of travel. With us, as also on all the many journeys, to Bsherri, to the ancient city of Damascus, and elsewhere, went David Azrak, the young science professor from the American University, to whose tireless kindness, interest, and ingenuity we owe the most and the best of all that we saw in that country of Gibran. It was he who planned our days after we learned that a return to America was imperative, he who was our interpreter and our guide and, more than all, our friend in the finest sense of the word up to the moment that we took our way to the pier on our day of departure.

On that last Sunday, David and Christopher and I went to the College de la Sagesse, once Al-Hikmat. We saw all that had been done in the interest of educating the young Lebanese to the rich traditions and culture of the Arabic world. And there, passing down a long cloister with the Abbé Jean Maroun, a tall, lean, dark-eyed, reverent man, we saw a little shabby old door, low and drab, looking decidedly out of place amidst all that was new and modern and elegant.

The Abbé stopped and put his hand on the knob of the door. And David said, "It is the room where Gibran worked and studied in his youth. They call it 'the heart of the College.' They have not allowed a thing to be changed. The new College was built around this room."

We entered. The old room, indeed. Old desks, hacked by knives of students long ago. The old desk where Father Haddad had sat — the only man who had ever taught Gibran anything. The old blackboard. And the Abbé put a piece of chalk in the hand of the little child, who knows and loves his friend Kahlil "in the mist" — and the child wrote on the blackboard some markings of his own. And no one spoke.

The next evening, the night before our sailing, a group of these gracious people came to our hotel. They did not come for my sake alone, but in remembrance of this man from Lebanon. I write it so you may know that they were paying homage in every way they could to the memory of their countryman, who had lived most of his life in our country, and had died here, leaving a legacy of untold and immeasurable treasure to our world and theirs.

There came David Azrak, Colonel Midawwer, Yusef Hoyiek, the sculptor, Edmund Wéhbé, of the French High Commission, Fouad Boustany, journalist and authority on Arabic literature, the Emir Maurice Chehab, Curator of the National Museum, and, to my great joy, President Bayard Dodge of the American University and Mrs. Dodge, those friends who had made a difficult situation less difficult and given us so many quiet hours of pleasure in their lovely garden.

We talked of Gibran, of course, and of my returning after the war, of what might be done to make the inheritance from the poet of the most value to all who would wish to benefit thereby.

Then *bon voyage*, and the chapter was closed.

Late that evening I went out alone and stood upon the terrace of the quaint little hotel with the big name, the Grand Hôtel d'Orient Bassoul, close to the water, the beautiful bay of Saint Georges, at the corner of the rue Chateaubriand and the rue Française. I said these words over to myself, the lovely French names, feeling a strange reluctance to leave Beirut, to leave Lebanon. I had come with the desire to spend several years, to make a study of the Arabic so that I might translate. I had hoped to give the child the beginnings of his education here. I wanted to hear him speak the Arabic words in his childhood, to sing the Arabic songs, to live in the atmosphere that Gibran had been part of.

Bsherri had seemed to me the essence of simple beauty

and rightness, for us. To have lived part of the year in Bsherri, part of the year in Beirut!

But war had come. I looked across the bay to the mountains. They seemed to be the embodiment of peace eternal, lying under the great pendent stars that crowded the blue night sky.

Then suddenly . . . America! Home! I thought of all I had left, the most dearly beloved ones, my own, and my heart suddenly gave a surge of joy. And I was glad to know that on the morrow we would go home.

It was America that Kahlil Gibran had chosen for his home. Here he had elected to live out his years and to bring to completion the labours of his life and his love. America had received him with sincere and generous acclaim. America will not forget Gibran.

And it may well be that here, rather than in Lebanon, the power of his words and his works shall find the widest, deepest channel, shall become a river of refreshing to a barren and devastated world.

In our own West, across this continent in the great tower of the Shove Memorial Chapel at Colorado College is a set of Westminster chimes cast at Croyden, England, with a master bell weighing six tons, which will strike the hours. And upon this bell are graven the words,

YESTERDAY IS BUT TODAY'S MEMORY,
AND TOMORROW IS TODAY'S DREAM.

KAHLIL GIBRAN

CHRONOLOGICAL TABLE

1883. Gibran Kahlil Gibran was born on January 6 at Bsherri, Lebanon.

Was tutored at home, learning to speak Arabic, French, and English.

1894. Came to Boston with his mother, his half-brother, and his two younger sisters.

1896. Returned alone to Beirut, where he matriculated at the Madrasat Al-Hikmat [School of Wisdom]. Studied a great variety of subjects outside of the prescribed curriculum, including medicine, international law, the history of religion, and music.

1901. Concluded his courses of study with high honors. During this period he had written the first version of *The Prophet* at fifteen, had edited a literary and philosophical magazine, *Al-Hakitat* [The Truth] at sixteen, had made his first appearance in public print, a prose poem in a Mt. Lebanon newspaper, at seventeen, and at the same age had made drawings of several pre-Islamic poets of whom no portraits existed, i.e., Al Farid, Abu N'was, Al Mutanabbi, and Avicinna, of Ibn Khaldun, the historian, Ibn Sinna, philosopher, and Khansa, the greatest Arabic woman poet. After obtaining his degree he visited Greece, Italy, and Spain en route for Paris.

1901–03. Studied painting in Paris. Wrote profusely in Arabic during these two years. Wrote *Spirits Rebellious,* which was burned in the market-place in Beirut soon after publication. For the writing of this book Gibran was exiled from his country and excommunicated from the Maronite Catholic Church, the book having been pronounced "dangerous, revolutionary, and poisonous to youth."

1903. Was called to America by the deaths of his half-brother and his youngest sister, and by the fatal illness of his mother. He reached his mother upon her death-bed. He was now left with one sister, Marianna, in Boston.

1903–08. Painted and wrote in Arabic, in the Syrian quarter in Boston, and his pictures began to attract serious attention. During this time he rewrote *The Prophet* in Arabic. Exhibitions were held at the Studio of Fred Holland Day, a well-known photographer, and his first patron (January, 1904), the Cambridge School, a private educational institution conducted by Miss Mary Haskell, who became Gibran's close friend and benefactress (February, 1904), and again in the Fred Holland Day studio later in the year, when the building burned, destroying the entire collection of drawings and paintings (1904).

1908. Went to Paris (visiting London en route) to study at the Académie Julien, and at the Beaux Arts.

185

1908. Received information that his exile had been remanded when the "new government in Turkey . . . pardoned all exiles."

1908–10. Met and made portraits of numerous distinguished persons in Paris, among them, Rodin, Henri de Rochefort, Debussy, Maurice Maeterlinck, the younger Garibaldi, and Edmond Rostand. Exhibited twice in the Paris Salon.

1910. Returned to Boston, Spring. Later in the year took residence in New York City at 51 West Tenth Street, the first studio building ever to be built in this country for the exclusive use of painters and sculptors. Lived in this building until his death.

1910–17. Exhibitions were held at the Montross Galleries, New York, in December, 1914, the Knoedler Galleries, New York, in 1917, and at the Doll and Richards Galleries, Boston, in April, 1917.

1917–22. During this period Gibran rewrote *The Prophet*, still in Arabic. He wrote several Arabic books: *Broken Wings*, in novel form; *The Tempests*, prose poems; *The Book of Tears and Laughter* and *Nymphs of the Valley*, prose poems, and *Processions*, a book-length narrative poem in strict Arabic rhyme and rhythm. Also a volume was published called *Al Badayih wal Tarayiff* [Beautiful and Rare Sayings], in which volume were published the drawings of the pre-Islamic poets and writers, drawn from imagination at 17. *Processions* is profusely illustrated with a series of drawings

186

employing a master technique of draughtsmanship, together with intensely mystical concepts.

1922–29. During this period two exhibitions were
held, one at the Woman's City Club, Boston, in January,
1922, the other at the Hotel Brevoort, New York, in
January, 1929. Also during this period portraits were
made of many distinguished persons, among whom were
Lady Gregory, Sarah Bernhardt, William Butler Yeats,
Dr. Charles Eliot, Richard Le Galliene, Paul Bartlett,
John Masefield, Leonora Speyer, Edwin Markham,
Abdul Baha, AE [George William Russell], Laurence
Housman, Johan Bojer, Witter Bynner, Ruth St. Denis,
Josephine Preston Peabody, and Alice Raphael. Two
original wash drawings and three pencil drawings are
in the Metropolitan Museum, New York, a number in
the Fogg Museum, Cambridge, Massachusetts, in the
Brooklyn Museum, and in the Newark Museum. A col-
lection of wash and pencil drawings is in the possession of
Barbara Young, Gibran's literary executor. This col-
lection has been exhibited widely in American cities, in
England, and has had a showing in Paris.

1931. Gibran died at St. Vincent's Hospital, New
York, on April 10. His body lay in a funeral parlour for
two days, and thousands of persons came to say their
farewell. The body was then taken to Boston, where it
lay in state, with bodyguards from his native Bsherri.
A funeral service was conducted in the little Church of
Our Lady of the Cedars; thence the body was taken

187

to a vault to await the journey to Lebanon. In July the body was taken aboard ship after a service on the pier at Providence, and was carried to Beirut, and then to Bsherri, where the casket rests upon a bier in the grotto adjoining the Monastery of Mar Sarkis, the crypt chapel of the Monastery.

A NOTE ON THE TYPE IN
WHICH THIS BOOK IS SET

✧✧✧✧✧✧✧

This book is set on the linotype in Caslon, so called after William Caslon (1692–1766), the first of a famous English family of type-designers and founders. He was originally an apprentice to an engraver of gun-locks and gun-barrels in London. In 1716 he opened his own shop, for silver-chasing and making bookbinders' stamps. The printers John Watts and William Bowyer, admirers of his skill in cutting ornaments and letters, advanced him money to equip himself for type-founding, which he began in 1720. The fonts he cut in 1722 for Bowyer's sumptuous folio edition of John Selden, published in 1726, excited great interest. A specimen sheet of type faces, issued in 1734, made Caslon's superiority to all other letter-cutters of the time, English or Dutch, quickly recognized, and soon his types, or types modelled on his style, were being used by most English printers, supplanting the Dutch types that had formerly prevailed. In style Caslon was a reversion to earlier type styles. Its characteristics are remarkable regularity and symmetry, as well as beauty in the shape and proportion of the letters; its general effect is clear and open, but not weak or delicate. For uniformity, clearness, and readability it has perhaps never been surpassed. After Caslon's death his eldest son, also named William (1720–78), carried on the business successfully. Then followed a period of neglect of nearly fifty years. In 1843 Caslon type was revived by the then firm of Caslon for William Pickering and has since been one of the most widely used of all type designs in English and American printing.

PRINTED BY HALLIDAY LITHOGRAPH CORPORATION, WEST HANOVER, MASS. BOUND BY THE BOOK PRESS, BRATTLEBORO, VERMONT.